EXTRADITED!

One Man's Prison Hell
and His Lover's
Fight for Justice

JOHN PACKWOOD & JANE AMESTOY
with Andrew Crofts

First published in 2007 by Vision,
a division of Satin Publications Ltd
101 Southwark Street
London SE1 0JF
UK
info@visionpaperbacks.co.uk
www.visionpaperbacks.co.uk
Publisher: Sheena Dewan

© John Packwood and Jane Amestoy 2007

A catalogue record for this book is available from
the British Library.

ISBN HB: 978-1-905745-06-7
Export PB ISBN: 978-1-905-745-128
2 4 6 8 10 9 7 5 3 1

Cover and text design by ok?design
Printed and bound in the UK by
Mackays of Chatham Ltd, Chatham, Kent

To Catherine

FOREWORD

By the time I retire from the law, I expect I may have forgotten many of the faces that have stared out of foreign prison cells seeking help. But certain memories never fade. I can still picture John Packwood at Kenitra prison, just off a dusty road in a nowhere part of Morocco.

Johnny was in the Moroccan jail after losing his year-long extradition fight from Spain. In 1997 he, along with three other sailors from the Isle of Wight, responded to an advert and subsequently delivered an ex-British naval boat to Morocco for the new owner. Unbeknown to the hapless crew, customs and the boat's broker and seller, the new owner was part of the infamous Cali Cartel. More than ten weeks later, a new Columbian crew were caught off the coast of Agadir with 6 tons of cocaine, which they later admitted had been placed on the boat just before they were caught. This was and still is the largest cocaine seizure in Moroccan history.

Every stone was unturned by Morocco in order to capture as many members of the cartel as possible. The local judge assigned to the case believed that the English crew that delivered the boat ten weeks earlier must have been part of the cartel. Despite no supporting evidence other than that they had delivered the boat, international arrest warrants were issued against them. By analogy, it was tantamount to seeking to arrest the previous user of a hire car after the subsequent user of the vehicle was caught with drugs in it. The British authorities, aware of the warrant, reached the obvious conclusion that the crew were clearly innocent and took no action. The only official advice Johnny received was simply not to travel to Morocco.

Seven years later, Johnny went to Spain with a friend for a short holiday. It would prove to be the worst holiday of his life. After the shock of being arrested by the Spanish, Johnny then discovered that Spain had a bilateral extradition treaty with Morocco. After almost a year battling extradition, members of his family were recommended to get in touch with me.

It was not perhaps the best of times for me to get involved, as his position seemed hopeless, regardless of a superb team of advisers that had done everything that was possible in an uphill struggle. It was now time to start focusing on evidence rather than technicalities. We had to begin corroborating Johnny's innocence and therefore commence the ever difficult task of proving a negative. I always knew we would get Johnny home, I just didn't know how or when and, more importantly, how much longer he would last. I have acted for many

UK prisoners in remote prisons and one of the hard calls is deciding how long one has to get them out before they crack, kill themselves or get killed. I sensed that with Johnny I had more time than I could expect from the average person, but I knew a year in the high-security terrorist prison in Spain would have taken a psychological toll.

After leaving court one day, I gave an interview to the BBC, venting my disbelief at the justice system. I was extremely angry at what had happened and realised that we had to make the Moroccans realise that Johnny Packwood would not be forgotten. I called my wife, Mariella Frostrup, a writer and TV presenter, and she agreed to help me pursue a cunning plan. I telephoned my friend, George Clooney, and explained the shambolic state of affairs and told him we were going to start a campaign for a man no one had ever heard of. George said he was in and it was not long before other friends such as Damien Hirst, Mark Knopfler, and Hugh Grant were similarly signed up.

Seeing Johnny's face as he came through Heathrow made it a fine day. I am so grateful for all those that supported Jane's campaign and helped see that justice was done. There are simply too many names to mention. I only wish they could all have been there to witness his return. Lurking unannounced in the shadows that day, far from the press, was Damien Hirst, who had dropped by to witness the result of a campaign that he was so instrumental in. My wife too deserves special thanks, not just for gathering the campaign team together but for letting me go to defend Johnny in Kenitra, four days after our son was born.

This book is not just a tribute to the bravery and courage of one man, but also a tribute to the inherent spirit of individuals, whatever prison they may dwell in around the world, that are rightly fighting without compromise for justice and their innocence. Johnny should be a pin-up for such people – he kept his dignity and faith throughout – and give them hope to fight on. This story also stands as an example of how human beings will gather to support another in their darkest hour. For as Edmund Burke said, 'The only thing necessary for the triumph of evil is for good men to do nothing.'

Jason McCue
H_2O Law

INTRODUCTION

John

In March 1997 a friend asked if I fancied a job as the engineer on a boat delivery to Morocco. I had worked with Matt before, having spent five weeks delivering a boat to Cyprus when he was just a deckhand. Now he was a newly qualified captain and I liked the idea of working with him again. He had found the job through an internet recruitment agency, which was how most of those delivery jobs were advertised.

The *Cygnet* was a shabby old ex naval patrol ship from the 1970s, once under the command of the Princess Royal's husband, Commander Tim Laurence, and the Navy had been trying to offload it for three years. She was basically a gun ship, although the guns were removed. At 42 metres long and weighing 240 tons, she was easily the biggest boat I had ever delivered. At the time she was valued at £120,000. She had been sitting in dock in Southampton and someone had finally shown an interest in buying her.

When Matt and I went over to look at her we could see that she was in a pretty bad shape, but we were confident she would be able to make the journey if we nursed the old engines along carefully enough. I was nervous at the thought of being the only engineer on the trip – it would obviously be down to my skills as to whether or not she was going to make it, but it seemed like a challenge and an adventure too exciting to miss.

We met the broker who was selling her on behalf of the Royal Navy and he showed us around, telling me of some of her little quirks. It was obvious that several things had to be done on the boat before we could leave harbour after being laid up so long, but they didn't seem beyond our capabilities. We were introduced to the businessman who was buying the boat from the broker. He told us he was Spanish and was planning to repaint the *Cygnet* white and use it as a pleasure cruiser.

'So why Morocco?' we asked.

'Because the labour is cheap and we can refit her there.'

It doesn't matter what colour you paint her, I thought, she's still going to look like a knackered-out old gun ship. But although it seemed a strange choice of vessel for pleasure cruising, it was not my job to criticise. You hear a lot of hare-brained schemes in the boating world so there was no reason not to believe that he was sincere in his plans.

I had listened to enough sailors' stories over the years to know that Morocco could be a bit of a dodgy country when it came to smuggling. Because of its geographical location – midway between the cocaine-producing countries in the Middle East and the consumers in Europe – it often found itself included on the itineraries of criminals like drugs and arms dealers. But I had never been there myself and had no more than anecdotal evidence. We didn't think there was anything dishonest about the deal since the sale was being made by the British government through a yacht broker. The Royal Navy wouldn't be selling the boat to anyone they thought was a criminal, would they?

All the arrangements were very friendly and casual. We didn't even think to have contracts drawn up since we weren't going to be paid a great deal of money. The sort of businessmen who buy boats like this on a whim can usually pay people like me out of their back pockets. It simply isn't worth the bother trying to cheat us.

Just as a matter of course, we gave the boat a thorough search from top to bottom – partly to make sure she was sea worthy and not storing up any nasty little surprises that would come to light in the middle of the ocean and partly to ensure there was nothing hidden that we might be accused of exporting from England or importing to Morocco. We didn't think there would be any drugs (after all, who has heard of people smuggling drugs *into* Morocco?) but we wanted to make sure there weren't any guns or anything else that might get us into trouble when we got to the other end.

The ship was old and the engines were not in brilliant shape, having been lying idle for three years, but I was pretty sure I could keep them going long enough for the voyage. I knew the Navy would have taken good care of her during her years of service. The new owner was planning to overhaul her when she got to Morocco so he wasn't going to spend a lot of money on the engines in England. It sounds irresponsible now, but in a way the run-down state of the ship added to the excitement of the adventure ahead. Nursing her along would be a challenge to our seamanship.

As the day of departure drew closer, we studied the charts for the voyage and planned the weather, wanting to avoid the worst of the seasonal storms. We decided to leave Southampton on 2 April and laid in enough supplies for the trip. I found two young guys who would be willing to be our deckhands, Ollie and Henry. In hindsight, we probably should have had a crew of six for a ship that size. Even though we were all competent sailors, two more men would have meant we could have taken shorter watches, but we thought we could get away with four as we didn't foresee any problems. The owner had told us he would also be sending his own representative, who could be helpful as a radio operator, on the trip. (We were later to discover that the man, Vincente, didn't speak a word of English, and if he was operating any radio I never saw it. In fact, he spent most of his time below in his cabin.)

The day before we were due to leave, Matt rang me.

'I'm really sorry,' he said, 'I've been waiting for a hospital appointment for months for some tests and it's finally come through. I can't afford to pass it up. I'm not going to be able to go.'

By then I had got excited about the idea of the voyage and making some money, and I wouldn't have been able to find anything else at such short notice. It might only have been £100 a day plus expenses, but I needed it just to meet my mortgage repayments for the coming months.

'But if you can find another captain,' Matt said, 'there's no reason why you shouldn't still make the trip.'

My home town, Cowes, is full of sailors, many of whom are out of work on any given day, so I put the word out around the pubs that I was looking for someone and a chap called Colin came forward to volunteer. I knew him and I knew he was a good captain, so I had no hesitation in recommending him to replace Matt. Colin spoke a little bit of Spanish too, so could easily communicate with the new owner. The crisis had been averted and the adventure was still on.

The problem with taking a ship out to sea is you can never just pull over and put on the handbrake, like you can with a car or a truck. However tired you might be, whatever problems you encounter, you have to keep going. With four of us in the crew (not counting the owner's representative, who didn't seem interested in playing any part in the running of the ship), we could divide the day up into four six-hour watches with either Colin or me awake at all times and with one of the deck-hands for support. If everything went smoothly it wasn't going to be a problem. Everything did go well until we reached the Bay of Biscay on the second or third day, where we ran into a powerful wind.

The worst thing about meeting bad conditions is what it does to your stomach, and we all started to suffer from seasickness as the *Cygnet* was tossed about – up, down and from side to side. Most experienced sailors can get sick at the start of a trip like that and just ride it out (apparently Nelson was always sick for the first couple of days after leaving port and would then get used to the roll of the ship), but this was much worse than usual. The *Cygnet* was top-heavy anyway, having a crow's-nest and flying bridge, and it was rolling horribly. The engines were also suffering from the storm; all the sediment that had been lying in the bottom of the fuel tanks for the previous three years was being shaken up, mixing with the fuel and blocking the filters.

Every two or three hours the revs on one or other of the two 2,000 horsepower engines (each about 6 metres long and 3 metres wide) would begin to drop and threaten to cut out. I would have to run down to the engine room before it died completely and switch over to a clean filter. If it died I knew I would have to restart it, and I also knew the batteries were old and might give out at any moment.

Most of the times this happened I would catch it just before it was about to stutter to a halt and it would rev back up again to a steady beat as the fuel started to flow cleanly again. On the times when I got to the engine room too late and one of the engines failed, I would struggle to restart it and the life in the batteries ebbed a little further away each time. They wouldn't hold the charge I was feeding them, being too old and feeble. I knew that I probably only had a few more chances before I would be unable to get any spark of life out of them at all.

Even when I tried to get some sleep half of my brain was listening to those revs; I was always poised to make another quick dash, my stomach heaving with seasickness. Exhaustion was threatening to overwhelm me, but I couldn't give in to it. I had to keep the ship going. The few times I did manage to fall into a deep sleep, I was always dragged back to consciousness by the shouts of the others, telling me that either the port or starboard engine was going again and I would drag myself off my bunk and back onto my feet. The engines had the names 'Jake' and 'Elwood' printed on them by the Navy sailors, so when emergency struck I would hear the shouts, 'Elwood's gone!' or 'Jake's losing power!'

We only had limited spares filters with us so I had to clean the dirty ones out in a bucket by hand each time I changed them, getting covered in evil-smelling diesel, which I could never fully clean out of my skin – no matter how hard I tried. Despite all this extra work I still had to take my turn on the bridge steering the vessel in order to give Colin a chance to sleep as well. We hardly saw Vincente, the so-called radio operator, at all. He had been in his cabin the whole time, no doubt feeling as ill as the rest of us. We didn't think about him that much, having all our time taken up with just keeping the ship and ourselves going.

By day five of the trip the inevitable happened and one of the batteries fell silent and lifeless, leaving us functioning on one engine. We were left chugging along at about eight knots, half the speed we should have been achieving, and it now became even more crucial that the last engine was not allowed to die.

Since there was now a real possibility we would break down, we had moved right out to sea, about 300 miles from the coast. That way if the worst happened and we lost both engines we would have plenty of space to drift until someone came to rescue us before we were shipwrecked. The storms passed and we continued to limp along at half speed, constantly listening for the sound of the last engine failing.

It was becoming increasingly obvious we couldn't get much further, so when we drew level with the port of Agadir, Colin radioed ashore in his best Spanish and asked if we could come into port to make repairs. The port we were heading for was a good bit further on and there was a strong chance we wouldn't make it. The authorities, however, were not in the mood to cooperate. We were too big a vessel to make a surprise visit, they told us. They needed notification before they could accept us. But the engine was coughing and spluttering now and I was sure we couldn't get as far as our destination. We headed inland regardless.

'If we drop anchor and switch off the engine,' I suggested to Colin, 'then they'll have to rescue us and tow us in. It's our only choice.'

Colin nodded his agreement and killed the engine. After having spent so long listening to the revving, the silence was a shock. We sent out our request for help as the *Cygnet* bobbed helplessly up and down in the swell, and we settled down to wait for assistance.

The hours passed slowly and we felt very alone, staring out at the empty sea around us. We caught up with our sleep, ate what was left in the galley, and talked. There was still no sign of the 'radio operator' emerging from his cabin. For twenty-four hours nothing happened. Our constant attempts at making radio communications for assistance were proving fruitless. It was beginning to look as if they weren't going to respond and now I wasn't sure that we would be able to get the engine started again, even if we wanted to. It felt like someone had decided to teach us a lesson.

Finally we spotted some ships approaching over the horizon, five or six or them, apparently racing to get to us first. We went out onto the deck to watch them turn from distant specks into recognisable vessels. As they got closer we could see that only one of them was the official coastguard. The crews on all the other boats were shouting at us, chucking lines over the side for us to catch.

'Don't throw them the lines,' the coastguard shouted at us. 'They'll be after salvage money.'

We obediently threw the coastguards our line and they pulled us into the port. We certainly didn't want to incur salvage bills for our employer, especially as we had now failed in our mission to deliver the boat to his chosen port and there was a strong possibility he would dock some of our pay. Once they realised they weren't going to get our business the other ships turned back and we all headed into Agadir in a flotilla.

The owner, who had flown down to Morocco to meet us, was waiting on the quayside as we were towed in, and he was not a happy man at the thought of his newly purchased boat having to be rescued at sea. I guess he felt the British Navy had ripped him off, and he may well have had a point. As he marched onto the gangplank he was surrounded by about fifteen men in uniform, all shouting orders at once, telling us to stay on the boat until they had searched it. Anyone would have thought we'd turned up in a nuclear submarine and were planning some sort of invasion. There were men from Customs and Excise, harbour officials and police, all vying to exercise their little bit of power and influence. They poured on board and spread out through the boat, searching it from top to bottom, end to end. We all sat with the owner and the police captain in the mess area, making them tea, while his minions did the searching.

'You'll need to get those fuel tanks drained and cleaned out before you start using this boat for anything commercial,' I told the owner. 'And you need a new set of batteries before you go anywhere.'

He listened intently and nodded his understanding. It didn't seem to me as if he had the slightest interest in any of the technical details, he was just impatient to get his hands on his new boat.

Although the officials didn't expect to find anything, they still spent between four and six hours on the search. During their many breaks they went straight to the giant stainless steel fridge in the mess area and seemed mildly offended that there weren't cakes and sweets waiting for them, just a nearly-empty tub of margarine. Because we'd been at sea for several days longer than expected our supplies had completely run out and we had nothing to offer them beyond cups of tea. We couldn't understand why it was taking so many of them so long to do a straightforward search. Over the next few days we learnt that to get anything done with officials like these at any speed you need to offer them gifts, even if it is no more than a packet of cigarettes. When we were finally free to drive out of the port area in the owner's car, for instance, we couldn't understand why the guards just left us sitting there, waiting.

'Anyone have cigarettes?' the owner asked.

One of us gave him a few packets of cigarettes, which he handed out through the car window.

'Is that all?' the guard asked before the barrier duly lifted.

So that was how it was done. It was a relief to be finally driving away from the ship with the job now behind us, and I was looking forward to having a nice bath before sinking into a comfortable hotel bed for an uninterrupted night's sleep. The owner drove us to the hotel and booked us in, promising to come back the next day with our money and plane tickets home. We'd originally thought we would spend a few days in Morocco, having a mini holiday before flying back, but the trip had been so arduous we all just wanted to get home as quickly as possible.

Once the owner had gone and we were on our own in the hotel it occurred to us that there was nothing to stop him from disappearing without paying us. We could hardly take the boat back as collateral now – it was moored in the port and we wouldn't have had a clue how to set about finding him. We realised we had been naïve in not asking for at least part of our money up front, but it was too late to do anything about it now; we had no choice but to trust him.

Once he'd left we bathed and changed and decided to go out to a restaurant for a meal. With some decent food and drink inside us we began to feel more human as we made our way wearily back to our beds. The part of the city we were in seemed to be a building site – dusty, noisy and unattractive. As we wandered through the dirty streets we heard the sound of blows and a woman screaming at the top of her voice. The sounds were coming from a police sentry box. As we drew closer we could see through the open door into the lit interior, where a policeman had taken his belt off and was thrashing a woman in black who was cowering on the floor.

'Hey!' I protested, stepping towards the door, but Colin caught my arm, holding me back as the policeman looked up angrily to see who was daring to remonstrate with him, his arm raised and ready to strike again.

'Don't get involved,' Colin hissed. 'That's the way things are done around here. She could be a prostitute or something. You don't know the whole story.'

The scene seemed to typify the dirt and squalor of the place and I felt even keener to get back to the safe, clean greenery of spring back at home on the Isle of Wight.

The next morning our fears proved unfounded and the owner was back at the hotel with the agreed payment of £800 each and, more importantly, tickets for us to fly out of Agadir airport in two days' time.

We all looked at one other, knowing we were thinking the same thing.

'Are there any earlier flights?' I asked, using Colin to loosely translate. 'Only we're keen to get back home.'

'Okay,' he said, apparently as anxious to get us out of the country as we were to be gone, 'I'll find out.'

He came back an hour or two later to tell us that he could get us a flight out of Casablanca first thing the following morning. The only problem was we would have to spend the night in the airport. By that stage we didn't care. We certainly weren't keen to spend any more time in Agadir, so he piled us into his uncomfortable, beaten-up little car and drove us the 300 miles to Casablanca. No doubt he was pleased to save himself the cost of our hotel rooms.

We spent the night sitting and lying on the seats around the airport, watching the security guards and police wandering around with their guns holstered, holding hands, or sitting smoking with their arms round one another's shoulders. It seemed a strange country where the men were happy to beat their women but treated one another like lovers. I realised that this was a culture I understood nothing about.

When we arrived in Britain we hired a little car to drive back home from the airport, and I got stopped for speeding by the police. They said I was doing 92 miles per hour. I was surprised a car that small could do that speed. I was pretty angry at the time. It seemed like the icing on the cake, a bad end to a bad trip, but it would later be a useful piece of evidence that I was in Britain on that day.

CHAPTER ONE

John

I have always loved the Isle of Wight. My father was well known on the island, even though he hadn't been born or brought up there. He came from London originally, and my mother, Frances, came from Scotland, where they met and fell in love. Dad had always thought the Isle of Wight would be a nice place to bring up a family, so once they were married he built a house for her and brought her to the island. They fitted in well and my dad was very active in the community. He was President of the Isle of Wight Chamber of Commerce and was responsible for bringing a lot of commercial firms to the island. This didn't go down well with some people who preferred relying on the tourists who came in the summer months, but it was vital for the general prosperity of the island to diversify and provide year-round employment for the population. A civil engineer by trade and a town and county planner, he founded the Cowes–Deauville twinning association and was involved in many other organisations, gaining him a lot of respect. The Deauville connection meant we had a lot of holidays in France and we used it as a starting point for travelling all over Europe.

Dad even received an MBE for his voluntary services to the community, which included working with old and young alike. Every Christmas he would rent a hall and throw a party for deprived children, which he found rewarding, having been an orphan himself. I was very proud of him.

I was his first child and he was already fifty-six when I was born and had built a big family house for my mother when they got married and settled on the island. Mum was thirty-six when she had me, so I was brought up in a very stable, mature family. In many ways it was an idyllic childhood, and from as early as I can remember I was building rafts out of old tin baths and pushing them down to the sea, or making go-carts, which we could take out on the quiet lanes and side roads.

I wasn't very clever at school and it wasn't until I had grown up that anyone realised I was dyslexic, which explained why I had found classes so difficult. Teachers didn't really recognise the condition in the 1970s, at least not in our school, so they just thought I was bone idle and 'unwilling to learn'. I just assumed I was a bit slow. I was always made to sit at the back of the class and the teachers would use me as a warning to the others: 'If you don't work harder you'll end up like Packwood.'

When they could see school-leaving age approaching the school sent us 'backward' children on work experience courses. I spent a week at a garage, working as a tea boy and a week as a porter at the hospital. I liked the hospital experience and went on a nursing course once school was over, but after dressing my first bedsore my nursing career came to an end. Next I tried a course in horticulture, but that didn't fit either. About a year after leaving school I got a job at Yelf's Hotel, part of the Trust House Forte Group, as an apprentice chef, living in. After nine months of that I went to work in a local bakery and just concentrated on enjoying my teenage years, getting a motorcycle and going to clubs and pubs with friends.

When a car I was overtaking turned right unexpectedly I came off my bike and through the driver's window, breaking my femur and collarbone and ending up in hospital for three months. It left me with a big scar and for a few days they weren't sure I would pull through. Once I had made a full recovery, however, I had to find another job. My father had a friend who was a director of a company making oil pollution equipment and sent me to see him about an apprenticeship. At last I'd found something I was good at and enjoyed and I had found my way into the marine industry. By that time I was already getting pretty good with motorbikes and car engines, spending many happy nights in the garage with stripped-down gear boxes and engines, just exploring how they worked, and I knew that I was skilful with my hands. The training to be an engineer went well, with me passing all my exams easily. At the age of twenty-two, with a four-year City and Guilds apprenticeship in engineering under my belt, it was time to move on once more and see some of the world.

So I went to Israel, spending three years working on a kibbutz. When my father suffered a stroke I came back to England to support my mother and help with his care. It was terrible to watch a man who had been so strong and full of life fading away. Four months later he died. After the funeral, I returned to Israel. I had fallen in love with an Israeli girl and eventually she came back to the Isle of Wight and we married. The marriage unfortunately didn't work out and I returned to my old way of life, spending several months travelling around America with a friend, taking work as and when I could find it. I still loved marine engineering, and it allowed me to travel and live in other countries, like Saudi Arabia, where I looked after the engines in huge luxury yachts, supervising their workforces. Most of our time was spent dealing with clutches that had been burnt out by owners who had no idea how to get their massive boats in and out of the marinas. I tried living in London for a while too, but it was too expensive and I couldn't manage to get a foothold. I soon realised the big city life just wasn't for me.

Over the years I did a number of boat deliveries around the world, mostly going south to places like Gibraltar, Malta and Cyprus. On one occasion I was part of a crew delivering a boat to Stockholm, heading across the North Sea. It was a ten-day trip and we passed about 400 oil rigs, their escaping gases burning brightly over the sea under the night sky, reflecting off the black waters like a city scene in some science fiction film. On nights like that I loved my work and the varied lifestyle it provided for me, even if I did find it hard to make a steady living.

Wherever I went in the world and whatever adventures I had, I was always pleased to get back home to the island.

By October 2004 everything had come right for me. I had fallen in love with a beautiful woman called Jane – someone I'd known for years, but had only just got to know properly. I had found someone who I wanted to spend the rest of my life with and, thanks to the rise in property values, I finally had enough money to start up my own business. After years of living on the edge of debt, juggling credit card payments and overdraft limits, the pressure was off at last and I could get out of the rut I had been stuck in. Now I had sold my house and had a bit of capital, I was bursting with ideas. I had never had the luxury of having money before and it was an exciting feeling.

I wanted to finish off work on *Seamist*, the 43-foot wooden cruiser I was renovating. I'd been working on her for the previous fourteen years and still hadn't had a day out at sea on her. She was a lovely old gentleman's cruiser, built during the First World War as a supply vessel to Admiral Beatty's flagship *Lion* at Jutland, and converted in the 1920s. She was full of teak panelling and decking, leather upholstery and brasswork, all of which I'd had to strip out and clean off. I had no idea how much work she would need when I first bought her, but I just couldn't bear to see such a beautiful boat rot away. Once I started taking her to pieces I kept finding more little things that needed doing. Initially I thought I would spend a few years putting her right and then I would take her down through the canals of France to the Mediterranean, where I could do little pleasure cruises to make a living. I had imagined a beautiful life, set up in a port somewhere, charging £10 a head to take cruises in the morning and then relaxing and enjoying myself for the next couple of days, living off the profits. But it hadn't happened quite like that and I still hadn't finished her. I've always been a bit of a perfectionist with things like that – cars, bikes, boats. I thought I would work during the winters in order to be able to take a couple of months off in the summer to work on her, but it hadn't been possible in recent years and I was looking forward to getting back home to finally finish her off.

I also thought there was a gap in the market for a company making wooden-framed windows now that plastic windows were going out of fashion. The Isle of Wight is a big market for replacement windows with so many houses looking out over the sea, taking the full brunt of the winds and sea spray during the rough weather. Or maybe I would import storm-damaged boats from America, do them up and sell them. There were plenty of options, I just needed to get my thoughts in order before deciding what to do first. I decided to have a week's holiday with my friend Peter to get all my plans clear in my head before knuckling down to my new life.

Peter was an old friend, who over the years had been my boss at one stage, and my lodger at another. He had a flat in Tarifa in southern Spain, a town that boasts it is the 'windsurfing capital of Europe'. He had just sold it and needed to move his stuff out so I thought I would go down with him for a week, try some windsurfing and help him out. I've never been very good at dealing with extreme heat, so it suited me to go at the end of the season when the sun was cooler and the beaches less crowded, which was great for me as a novice surfer.

We booked some cheap easyJet flights from Gatwick to Malaga. The plane was due to arrive at nine in the evening, so we would be able to pick up a hire car, drive the 100 miles to the flat in Tarifa and still get time for a good night's sleep in preparation for an energetic week. Peter had promised to teach me to windsurf.

Once we arrived at Gatwick airport we were already getting ourselves in the holiday mood. I was enjoying my last bottle of Newcastle Brown before boarding. 'Wonder when I'll have my next,' I said, knowing we wouldn't be able to get any in Spain. We were a bit late answering the call to get on the plane and I quickly sent Jane one last text message before we headed off to the boarding gate, telling her how much I loved her and would be missing her in the coming week.

By the time we finally made it to the plane, most of the other passengers were already boarded and seated and Peter and I weren't able to get seats together. It wasn't a problem for us; we were going to be together all week so it made no difference whether we sat together or not over the next few hours on the plane.

As Peter was nearer to the exit door, when we landed he disembarked before me. I was still waiting to get out of my seat and recover my hand luggage from the overhead locker as I saw him getting off the plane. Of course, if he got through customs and on to baggage reclaim while I was still queuing to get my passport checked, there wouldn't be any difficulties; he could go on to find the hire car and pick me up once I came through.

By the time I got to passport control he had disappeared momentarily from sight. The queue was moving pretty fast – passengers just held their passports up and were nodded through by the officials. They hardly even seemed to be looking at the proffered documents as we shuffled steadily forward. I smiled at Pete in the queue, having no idea that things were about to go terribly wrong.

As I got closer to the desk I opened my passport at the relevant page and held it up to the window, just like everyone else, and then everything became a blur of confusion. Someone grabbed my arms from behind and I felt the cold hard steel of handcuffs going onto my wrists, cutting into me and hurting. I was pulled backwards out of the queue by several airport officials, without a word being said, and hustled through a door just a few feet away. Most of the people in the queue would have been unaware that anything had happened, although those closest to me looked shocked and surprised by the sudden flurry of activity.

It was as if I had simply been spirited away from the normal world into some sort of parallel existence, like a character in a children's fantasy.

As the door closed behind me all the bustle and noise of the airport outside were silenced and it was just me and the wordless officials. In front of me was an empty metal cage, divided into four sections, dimly lit and stinking of urine. There was a stone bunk in each quarter but nothing else. Throwing open the door to one of the sections they undid my cuffs and pushed me in, slamming and locking the door behind me. I tried protesting and asking questions but it was as if they couldn't hear me; they just looked straight through me as if I hadn't spoken. Nothing was said as my bag and passport vanished with the policemen and they left me sitting alone, trying to work out what had happened.

All I could think was that there must have been some sort of mistake. They must have thought I was someone else and once they realised they would come and let me out and I could get on with my holiday. In a few hours' time Peter and I would be having a drink and laughing about it. I assumed that when I didn't emerge from baggage reclaim Peter would start asking questions and come looking for me. He would be able to explain that I wasn't whoever they thought I was and we would be able to get on with our holiday. There was nothing else I could do until then, since there was no one there for me to talk to and try to explain what had happened.

I wasn't too downhearted because my life had been going so well up till that moment, and I was sure this was only a temporary hiccup.

Time was dragging by very slowly on my concrete bunk. I tried shouting once or twice – 'What's going on? I'm English!' – but my voice just echoed round the small iron cage and no one took any notice. I was beginning to worry about Peter and how he must be wondering what had happened to me. I wanted to get a message out to him, but I couldn't think of a way to do it if I couldn't attract anyone's attention.

After an hour or two I realised there was little chance that anyone was going to let me out that night, so I rolled my jacket up to make a pillow and lay down on the stone bunk to try to sleep, so I would be reasonably fresh when I finally got to Tarifa in the morning. I assumed that it was taking longer to sort me out because it was now late at night. Once everyone got to work in the morning and turned their computers on and made a few telephone enquiries the authorities would realise they had made a mistake. Despite reassuring myself with these thoughts, I still couldn't sleep. My head was swimming and confused.

Jane

Once I had got over the initial sadness of seeing Johnny off on his holiday, I was quite enjoying the idea of having a week to myself with my ten-year-old daughter, Freya. When you have a young child and a job, there are always so many demands on your days you often don't get as much time to be with them as you would like. It would also give me some time to do some of the things I wanted to do.

Peter phoned me the morning after they left for Spain. It was Saturday and I had taken the ferry from the island across the Solent to Southampton to do some shopping.

'I've lost him,' Peter said.

I had trouble trying to work out what he was saying at first.

'What do you mean, you've lost him?'

It sounded like the sort of scrape the two of them were always getting themselves into. I was slightly amused at the thought that they couldn't even manage a simple trip to Spain without messing it up.

Peter told me that Johnny hadn't come through the airport and that the last time he'd seen him was in the queue for passport control. When only Johnny's bags were left on the carousel, going round and round on their own, he had decided he needed to do something, so he had taken all their bags out of the terminal and found the car they had hired, assuming that by the time he did that Johnny would have turned up. But he hadn't.

After sitting outside the airport for hours in the car, Peter thought they must have missed one another in some way and decided that if he drove down to the apartment in Tarifa, Johnny would meet him there. I couldn't quite understand why he hadn't made at least some enquiries in the airport first, since it seemed very unlikely Johnny would have gone anywhere without his bags or Peter. There seemed no logic to the whole situation.

Just that morning I'd been joking with Frances, Johnny's mum, about how I was looking forward to having a girlie week while he and Peter were off playing in the sea in Spain.

Frances had come to rely on John a lot since her hips and knees had started to trouble her. She had always been a passionate Scottish country dancer, but now even walking gave her problems. Because we all lived in the same small town it was easy for us to pop in and see her once or twice a day to make sure she had whatever she needed, or just for a chat. I was happy to take on the job while Johnny was away; Frances and I had always got on well.

During the days, when Freya was at school, I had Badger, Johnny's RSPCA rescue dog, for company. Badger is an energetic, good-natured mongrel terrier, the sort of scruffy dog you see in virtually every movie and television commercial. She missed Johnny terribly whenever he was away, even though we had only had her for about six months. When he was there she would never leave his side.

'Never mind,' I told her when Johnny left for his flight, 'he'll be home soon.'

Johnny and I have always known each other. My parents had also come from the mainland and, like Johnny, I had been born on the Isle of Wight. I was the second child of four, with an older sister, Laura, and two brothers, Miles and Ned. We grew up in Gurnard, the next bay round from Cowes. It is a tiny seaside village and our days were spent in the open fields, woods and on the beaches.

Johnny is three years older than me so we didn't get to know each other that well when we were kids, but I knew who he was – he was the boy who lived close to the school. His younger sister, Catherine, was in the same year as Laura. The Isle of Wight is not big; if you drive all the way round the coast road you would only do a journey of about 60 miles, and many of the families have lived on the island for years, so pretty much everyone knows something about everyone else.

Our paths drifted apart after school. As soon as I left I went straight to college to study hairdressing and got off the island at the first opportunity, keen to explore the world. Like a lot of young people I headed to London and took a succession of jobs, including working for a small catering company that had a number of contracts including supplying food to the *Big Breakfast* team at Channel Four. It was an exciting time for the programme, with Paula Yates making headlines almost every day.

I also worked on a fabric stall in Petticoat Lane, which later moved upmarket to Covent Garden, although it was never as much fun as the original market where Arab customers used to turn up with suitcases packed with pound notes and long lists of materials they wanted to take home with them. A lot of other islanders lived around the East End at the time; they even had their own football team, Isle of Wight Exiles, so I never lost touch with my roots.

Wanting to explore further I went to Australia for a year, cutting hair and cooking, joining a funfair and travelling all the way up the east coast. It was a fun time, meeting all sorts of different people on the road, although there were also times of terrible boredom, spending fifteen hours at a time walking up and down in a trailer, handing out balls and prizes to customers.

It was hard coming back to the Isle of Wight at the end of that year of sun and warmth of Australia when my visa ran out. It was November 1993 and it felt like returning to the Arctic. I missed the sun and the people and the life I had created over there. I tried going back to London for a bit, but most of my friends had moved on by then and I realised that I wanted to do the same. Once I'd got over the culture shock of being back in a cold climate I returned to the Isle and moved to the next stage of my life by having my daughter, Freya, although my relationship with her father didn't last.

Although both Johnny and I were coming and going from the island over the years, and we knew nearly all the same people, our paths hardly ever seemed to cross. It was like we both belonged to two separate social circles, which only occasionally overlapped. I had seen him at virtually every party I had been to on the Island, but we were always busy talking with different people and never got round to finding out any more about each other. Then, in the spring of 2003, our social circles started to overlap more and we began to get to know one another better. The chemistry was instant and before we could even catch our breaths we found ourselves in a relation-ship that felt like it had always been meant to be.

I loved Johnny like no one I had ever met before, but I still thought he was a clueless prat for getting himself lost on a simple trip to Spain.

John

The next morning the police reappeared and unlocked my cell door. I assumed they were going to apologise for the misunderstanding and arrange for me to be transported to Tarifa. I was tired and stiff from a bad night's sleep on the hard concrete, still feeling fearful and confused. I tried to strike up a conversation and was met with completely blank stares. It didn't look as if anything had changed. I was going to have to wait a bit longer before they realised their mistake.

They gave me a carton of orange juice and gestured for me to drink it before they cuffed my wrists again and bundled me out through the back of the airport to a police car. Still no one was saying anything to me as the car swerved and bumped through the streets of Malaga to the police station. Rather than being alarmed, I was actually more annoyed that they were eating into my holiday time. I knew things would soon be straightened out, but I was frustrated by my own inability to communicate with them and explain their mistake.

Once we reached the station I was put into another cell while everyone around me jabbered to one another in Spanish. No one was in any hurry to process me but after a couple of hours of sitting, staring into space, I was taken upstairs to an office where an official asked for my name and date of birth.

'What's going on?' I kept asking.

'You have problem,' the officer grunted eventually. 'Passport. Problem.'

That was obviously as much information as he was willing to give, or as much as his grasp of English would allow. I couldn't understand what problem there could be with my passport that would warrant this sort of treatment in a European country. I'd travelled to any number of other countries on it and I knew it hadn't expired. I hadn't been to any countries that might make me seem like a terrorist, so what was worrying them?

I desperately wanted to get in contact with Jane, to let her know I was all right. I was missing her and wishing I had never agreed to come with Peter. And where was Peter? Anyway, why wasn't he trying to find me and explain everything? The police had given me back my mobile, which raised my spirits, but the network wouldn't work and they wouldn't allow me to make calls on any landlines. I asked for a pen and quickly copied some numbers down before my phone was taken away from me again. I felt isolated and frustrated, seeing another day of my holiday slipping away – the sun shining outside the window of the cell as if to rub it in.

That afternoon, as I strained to try to pick up any clues from the Spanish voices babbling around me, I heard the word 'Morocco' and something clicked into place in my brain. It was a memory from six or seven years before. I concentrated hard, trying to remember what exactly had happened. It had started with a phone call to my house in the Isle of Wight.

'This is British Interpol,' the voice had told me. 'We would like to discuss a boat delivery you made recently.'

'Really,' I was taken aback, 'which one?'

'It would be better to discuss it face to face. Can we have a meeting?'

I agreed to take the ferry across to Southampton and meet them on the quayside. As I got there I saw two men waiting in a silver Vauxhall Cavalier and went over. I asked them to show me some identification before I climbed in with them and they showed me some official-looking papers, but I didn't bother to read them in any detail. I couldn't imagine they would be anyone other than who they said they were. They looked like two typical plain clothes policemen.

I climbed into the back of the Vauxhall and they drove to a nearby pub. Once we were inside they ushered me to a corner seat and sat either side of me; maybe they want-ed to make sure I didn't try to make a run for it. They kindly bought me a bottle of brown ale and ordered me a meal, so it didn't seem like I was in any terrible trouble.

'Do you remember delivering a boat to Agadir in Morocco?' one of them asked.

'Yeah,' I said, happy to cooperate, 'I remember it well.'

'The same boat has been involved in a large seizure of cocaine,' he explained. 'What do you know about that?'

'I don't know anything about it,' I said. 'I just delivered the boat. It didn't have any drugs on it then because we searched it from top to bottom.'

By the time I'd finished telling my story to the two policemen from Interpol, we'd all finished our lunch. They seemed quite happy with my account of the voyage, and obviously didn't want to tell me any more about the drug seizure that the *Cygnet* had been involved in ten weeks later, once it had been renamed the *Duanas*.

'We may be in touch with you at a later date,' one of them said as they drove me back to the ferry, 'but if I was you I wouldn't go back to Morocco just at the moment.'

'No problem,' I laughed. 'I certainly don't have any plans to go back there.'

Interpol didn't make any effort to talk to Colin, Ollie or Henry, which made me think they had felt that I was telling the truth and didn't need to investigate the matter any further.

All this came back to me as I sat in the dingy cell in Malaga, trying to work out what was going on around me. I decided there was no cause to worry because I knew I was innocent and had nothing to hide. Once the Spanish authorities discovered that British Interpol were happy that I was innocent, they would have to let me go – after all we were all in Europe.

That evening, at about 8.00 pm, after siestas, work resumed and it was my turn. I was taken to a courtroom in handcuffs and allocated a lawyer, a woman who spoke enough English to be able to explain to me that my guess had been correct. It was about that trip on the *Cygnet*. The Moroccans, she explained, wanted to extradite me to their country so I could stand trial for supplying a boat for a drug deal. I felt very annoyed with Interpol for not warning me that my passport had an international arrest warrant put on it by the Moroccan government, but I was confident that no European country would ever extradite the citizen of another European country to a place like Morocco. Once they had checked the paperwork and realised I was a marine engineer, I told myself again, they would realise I was innocent of any crime and I would be released to go and find Peter.

The frustration of not being able to communicate properly with anyone, added to the tiredness after such a bad night's sleep and all the stress, made me feel quite tearful as I struggled to reason with them and convince them that they were making a mistake. No one seemed to be taking any notice of anything I was saying. It was almost as if they were all looking through me, assuming

I was guilty of being part of some evil drug-running operation, dismissing my protestations of innocence as the predictable cries of someone who was almost certainly guilty. I guess virtually everyone they arrested made the same claims to innocence, so why should they believe me more than any of the rest of them? I would just have to wait until the British authorities realised what was happening and came to my rescue.

Someone who spoke better English came to my cell to take all my details and could see that I was beginning to feel the strain.

'Morocco,' she tutted sympathetically, 'this is not good for you.'

CHAPTER TWO

Jane

Peter's mum had lived in Spain for a few years and spoke the language, so Peter rang her for advice on what he should do about tracking Johnny down. She contacted the British Embassy in Malaga to tell them he had vanished at the airport and to try to find out if they knew what was going on. She then reported back to Peter.

'They know all about it,' he told me later that day. 'They say he's been arrested. He's in a Malaga jail.'

'Arrested for what?' I asked, half shocked and half annoyed with Johnny. I assumed that he must have done something really stupid to get himself in so much trouble before he had even entered the country.

'They wouldn't give her any more details than that.'

At least now we knew where he was. I was certain he hadn't broken any serious laws, so I guessed he would be let out as soon as they realised there had been a mistake.

I waited for Peter to say what he was going to do next, but he fell silent and I realised that he was just giving me the information and handing over responsibility to me.

Once I'd hung up and thought for a moment I realised that things were a little bit more serious than had appeared at first. What if this wasn't just some prank that had gone wrong and Johnny wouldn't be let out with a rap over the knuckles? Maybe something had gone badly wrong and I needed to do something. But what? Who should I alert? Who should I go to for advice? Never in my life had I found myself in a situation like this and I didn't have a clue where to start sorting it out.

I decided I needed to get some help, or at least find someone I could talk to. I didn't want to worry Johnny's mum at this stage, not if I didn't have to, so I rang his sister, Catherine, who lived on the mainland, near Salisbury.

We didn't really know each other, although we had met once or twice, but I knew she was someone I could trust and depend on. Catherine had started out working for Trust House Forte in the 1980s and Johnny had confessed he had been quite jealous of her when she became one of their youngest-ever regional controllers and was given her own car and mobile phone. She had since moved on to become a successful tax accountant.

When I told her the story, or as much of it as I knew at that stage, she was as bewildered at what could have happened as I was.

'Typical Johnny,' she grumbled.

Even though we were uncomfortable about being in such uncharted waters, neither of us were too worried as we were sure he was innocent of whatever they were accusing him. We just had to work out the best way to get him out of the jail quickly. It seemed a shame that his holiday was being messed up because he had needed a break. Still, it would be yet another story for Johnny to tell in the pub when he did get home.

The weekend was then spent trying to contact the British embassies in Malaga and London, but this was to no avail as John had not given them permission to discuss his situation. This permission could not be obtained until the following Tuesday, when the consular official would be able to visit him.

John

I spent most of the day in the courthouse where I was only asked my name and to confirm whether or not we had indeed delivered the *Duanas*. I was then transported to the local prison in a van with six or seven other prisoners, who all looked like they were on their way to start serving sentences. They didn't look like the sort of guys who might be being held for a night or two while enquiries were being made, like me. I kept my eyes to the floor, unsure what the etiquette in such a group should be, but knowing I didn't want to get involved in any conversations that might lead to misunderstandings. By the time we arrived at our destination it was approaching midnight. The prison looked like a pretty big place looming up in the blackness above us as we emerged from the van into the glare of spotlights. One by one our handcuffs were removed and we were herded into a section called *ingresso*.

Ingresso, I soon discovered, is the area of a prison you go to when you first arrive and need to be processed, or when you are about to leave. It is the last stage before the outside world disappears and you enter a different universe. We were instructed to stand in a line on wooden slats in front of a high desk and to take off our clothes. I could only half understand the orders that the guards were growling and grunting at us, and so followed the lead of the other prisoners as they stripped naked and piled their clothes up on the desk where three officers were going through everything, looking for any contraband.

Once we were naked, officers had us squat so they could check we hadn't got anything hidden up there. It was as if all my dignity had been stripped off with my clothes and I had been reduced to being nothing more than an animal as I stood there, waiting for my next orders.

After about twenty minutes of peering and searching we were told to put our clothes back on and had our fingerprints and photographs taken. I was now beginning to feel like I really was a prisoner, no longer a temporary visitor in this scary new world. Once they had finished with the formalities we were marched off to the cells and thrown a bundle of blankets and a rock-hard lump of foam for a pillow. I was put in with a young lad called Antonio.

'Hi,' I said and he nodded back. It was obvious he couldn't speak a word of English, and I couldn't speak a word of Spanish.

There were two bunks and Antonio was already on the top one; beside them was a concrete table and a stainless steel toilet pan and sink.

Even though it was at least 4.00 am by then the noise level was deafening as the other prisoners shouted to one another through the barred windows, probably trying to find out who the newcomers were – whether they knew any of us and what we were in for. The whole place was buzzing, doors banging and keys rattling, making my tired nerves jangle as I tried to work out a safe way to behave.

Despite the language barrier, Antonio was interested in finding out why I was there and I drew him a little picture of a boat, sailing towards Morocco. Once I mentioned the word 'cocaine' he seemed satisfied that he knew all he needed to know about me. I could see that he rated me as an equal if I was a cocaine smuggler, so I didn't try to protest my innocence. I knew by then he wouldn't believe me anyway. I was still in the jeans and T-shirt I had been arrested in and he kindly lent me one of his T-shirts and a pair of jogging bottoms to use as pyjamas. I was grateful for even this small display of friendship in that hard, noisy, hostile environment. As I curled up on the bunk and tried to sleep, all I could think about was Jane back in Cowes. I wished I could wake up and find it had all been a dream and I was actually curled up in bed with her.

But the next morning the nightmare continued. I was moved out of *ingresso* and onto a wing containing about

200 people. I couldn't understand how things had managed to get this far. Why had no one turned up to help me? How could I possibly have gone from being a tourist on an easyJet flight to being a foreign prisoner in such a short time?

As I started to find the courage to talk to other prisoners I realised that about a quarter of them were British, and they all seemed to be in for smuggling, selling or using cocaine. Many of them seemed like caricatures of East End villains. There was one guy in particular, about fifty years old, with a bright red drinker's face, wearing a Hawaiian shirt and flip-flops, who made no secret of his taste for coke.

'I'll do as much as I can get down my face,' he rasped cheerfully.

To start with I tried to explain to everyone I spoke to that I was innocent and had got caught up in it by accident, but they obviously didn't believe me.

'Yeah, all right, mate,' they'd say with knowing looks. 'Save it for the judge.'

Some of them actually seemed quite happy to be there, accepting that spending time in prison was just 'part of the job'. At least I was able to speak my own language again, and understand what was being said to me, making me feel slightly less isolated and far from home.

There were a lot of Africans in the mix as well, illegal immigrants waiting to be sent home, or serving time for smuggling in one form or another. They always seemed to be talking all the time at the tops of their voices, like they were exchanging news across a busy village street, even if they were only a few feet apart. The constant noise and activity of the place were dizzying and went on twenty-four hours a day. There was never a moment of quietness or calm; no chance to be alone with your thoughts as you tried to adapt to the surroundings. There were a number of people there on remand, a bit like me, waiting to hear what was going to happen to them, all of them scared and unsure of what was going on in their lives. I was beginning to share that fear. What if no one ever showed up to help me? What if I just kept on being hauled in front of non-English-speaking courts? It might be days or weeks before the whole mess was sorted out and I would be able to get home. The notion of continuing my holiday was now long gone.

My new cell-mate was again called Antonio, but this time he was an old boy who had spent sixteen years of his life in jail and knew the system very well. He didn't speak English either and I went back to communicating in little pictures. Half the time he was stoned out of his mind on cannabis, which made him pretty amiable. I noticed a lot of the long-term prisoners wore permanently glazed looks from taking drugs, either illegal ones or legal ones prescribed for depression. Every day the nurse would come onto the wing to hand out little envelopes of pills and half the wing seemed to go up for them.

At that stage I wasn't that interested in finding out about anyone else's stories. My mind was filled up with thinking about how I was going to get out of prison as quickly as possible. I still hadn't been able to get through to Jane or anyone else on the outside, and I still hadn't had a change of clothes. In fact it would take eighteen days, and Peter making a scene at the British embassy in Madrid, before I received some.

As the days passed I began to get my bearings. There were sixteen blocks in the jail, with 180 prisoners in each. Two of these wings had a courtyard in between them, where we were all thrown during the day, like 400 kids in a giant playground, except there was nothing to play with, and nowhere to sit, so we all just mooched around or sat in the dirt, staring at our feet or talking. There was a sitting area inside, and another area where we ate, but both were off-limits most of the day. Three flags flew above the gate, one Spanish, one European Union and one I couldn't identify. There was so little to look at that even the sight of a strange flag was intriguing, giving me something to think about.

Hundreds of cell windows looked out over the court-yard, and everyone used it as their personal waste disposal area. It was like walking around a rubbish tip, kicking your way through discarded food, bottles, old socks, tin cans and cigarette ends. Everywhere there were lumps of spit because of the way the dust settled in all our throats, making us want to clear them and get rid of the result every few minutes. Everyone smoked all the time, partly because cigarettes were cheap and anxiety was high and partly because of the greatest enemy, boredom.

When the wind got up the litter would swirl and clatter noisily around, providing a welcome visual distraction during the day, but becoming yet another barrier to sleep at night. When I first found I had a cell in a block overlooking the courtyard, rather than one staring straight at a wall, I'd thought it would be an advantage, but the noise could sometimes be almost too much to bear.

The inmates were always fiddling with the electrics, cutting wires with razor blades, trying to rig up different gadgets in their cells, overloading an already strained system, so the lights were often going out. The guards must have got fed up with it, and often left them off for a couple of hours before flipping the trip switch back on. The anger would rise from the cells like the roar of an approaching train, the banging of tin cups against bars and angry shouting. No light, no television, no music, just blackness. It would drive them mad. Sometimes prisoners would set light to salted peanuts, which they would have bought from the shop during the day, the oil on the nuts burning like a child's night light for anything up to five minutes.

Not every day was bad, and sometimes, as I adjusted to the new pattern of my life, the smallest piece of good luck would enliven me ridiculously. One morning a Brit who was being released donated his towel to me as he left. The gift of a cast-off towel would never have made my day until I actually had to spend some time without one. I suddenly began to appreciate the most basic of life's comforts. Up till that moment my one and only T-shirt had had to double up as a towel. I would also be able to roll the towel up to add some bulk to my pillow.

Armed with my precious new possession, I had my first shower since leaving home six days earlier, but I still had to put my dirty clothes back on afterwards. It had been five days before I got round to washing my one pair of pants in the tiny cell sink as I had assumed each day that I would be released. While they dried I just had to go around without them. I had two small holes in my jeans where a back pocket had been ripped off, taking the studs with it, and I didn't like the idea of showing my bare arse so I found myself continually pulling down my T-shirt as I walked.

On one side of the courtyard was a glass hut where the guards sat and prisoners were allowed to make phone calls on phones that were passed through the window. When we got to the front of the queue we would give the guard the number we wanted to call. He would dial it and then pass over the handset. The first day I queued up was my first chance to try to make contact with someone from my normal life, someone who wasn't trapped in the same surreal nightmare I was struggling with. I gave him Jane's number and he dialled it, huffing and puffing all the time.

'Is no good,' he muttered, hanging up and looking towards the next person in the queue.

'Try this one,' I pleaded, handing over Catherine's number, aware that I was only allowed one call and that the men behind me were growing restless. I suspected the guard had misdialled but I didn't have the nerve or ability to challenge him.

The guard hesitated for a second and then took mercy, sighed, tutted and dialled again. 'No good.' He shook his head, hung up and waved for me to make way for the next man. My chance of speaking to the outside world was gone and I felt a surge of panic.

'Please,' I begged, passing over my mother's number, 'try this one.'

The queue was protesting loudly and for a moment I thought he wasn't going to do it, but he took mercy one more time and dialled. Mum picked up. He handed me the phone.

'Hello, dear,' she said innocently.

'I'm having troubles, Mother,' I confessed. 'I'm in Spain and I've ended up in prison.'

The familiar sound of her voice, coming down the line from the island that had always been home, broke through the defences I'd been hanging onto for days and the tears started, despite the noise of the impatient crowd that was swelling behind me. I can only remember having cried twice before in my life; once when my father died, and the other time when I crashed my first car, an American Mustang. I was nineteen years old at the time and I had saved every penny to buy it but I crashed into Yarmouth Bridge because I was showing off to my friend, spinning the wheels. Now I found myself in the same position – distraught and being comforted by my mother.

'Don't worry, dear,' Mum said, the same rock I remembered all through my childhood. 'We'll sort it out.' She must have been in shock, receiving such an unexpected piece of news out of the blue.

Desperate to stay attached to my old life for as long as possible, I managed to keep talking for my allotted five minutes, trying to explain where I was and that I didn't really know what was going on, before the guard cut me off and the next man pushed me out of the way to get his turn. I sloped off to a corner of the courtyard and slumped down with my head in my hands. I didn't get another chance at a phone call for three or four days, so I was going to have to find some other way to make contact with Jane.

When I sat down to start writing her a letter, I realised that it would be the first love letter I'd ever sent her. We'd never been apart for any length of time since we started going out. It seemed a strange place to be writing something so meaningful, sitting in a place where I was never on my own and never felt like smiling. With hindsight, I guess a letter home with all the news should have been my first priority, but I was sure I would be home before it arrived anyway.

When you have nothing to do all day but think, your mind brings up memories that have been buried for years. The thought of home, as I sat stranded in that alien prison world, was almost too painful to bear. Each day there would be a five-hour stretch when we would all be pacing around the courtyard outside (or the 'cage' as the other prisoners preferred to refer to it). There would be nothing to do but listen to other Brits' stories and tell them mine, learning all about prison lore from those who had far more experience than I hoped I would ever have. The atmosphere was tense with aggression as every-one weighed one another up and jostled for power. Every so often I would gaze up at the pokey little window of my cell and long to be back in the safety and security of those four walls, even though I had been longing to get out and see something different just a few hours before.

The first week passed and I realised that my biggest worry was no longer missing my windsurfing holiday. Peter was now back on the Isle of Wight and it had moved into the past. My worry now was how long would it be before I too could go home.

Jane

It was dawning on Catherine and me that Johnny wasn't going to just walk out of jail unless we did something about getting him some help. We had assumed that it would only be a matter of time before the obvious wrong that had been done to him would be righted, but we were beginning to realise that we couldn't rely on that happening automatically. It was just possible that this miscarriage of justice would result in him spending more time in incarceration unless we did something about it.

We couldn't understand why it wasn't obvious to the authorities that he was innocent, but since nothing was happening we assumed we had to be proactive if we wanted to wake them up to this. The fact that we hadn't even been able to speak to him made it all the more frightening. If it hadn't been for the one call he had managed to get through to his mother, Frances, we wouldn't have heard a single word from him since his last text to me at Gatwick a week before. It was like he had been spirited out of our lives. At the beginning of the week I had been looking forward to some time for Freya, and myself, but now we were both beginning to miss Johnny badly. We had only been together for a year and a half, but we had already become very close to each other. It almost felt as if a part of myself was missing.

Catherine and I were spending hours on the phone to one another, going over and over what we should be doing, talking, talking, talking. We often went round in circles but still found comfort in our shared worries. Once John had given his consent, the only advice the embassy could give Catherine, as his next of kin, was: 'Get him a lawyer, someone who understands the local system. You can't rely on the free duty one they will have given him. They'll be there for court hearings only, they won't do any work in between.'

'How do we do that?' she wanted to know. Neither of us spoke Spanish. The embassy were being very polite and doing everything by the book, but I suspect they thought he was likely to be guilty, since there were so many Brits up on drugs charges of one sort or another. One more arrested drug smuggler must have seemed commonplace to them. The fact that the Moroccans wanted to extradite him to their country probably made it seem all the more likely that he was guilty. Why would they be going to so much trouble if he was innocent?

However, they still had to go through the motions of helping us, whatever their private opinions at the time.

'We can send you a list of names,' they said, 'but you will have to make the final choice yourselves.'

The list arrived and we started phoning them, with no idea which would be good and which would be useless. The fear of Johnny being extradited to Morocco, a country that sounded even more hostile to us than Spain, spurred us on to make the difficult phone calls. Some just didn't speak any English, so we couldn't take it any further. There was only one of them who seemed to think she could do anything to help.

'I am an expert in matters of extradition,' she said.

Her name was Inés Barba Novoa and she spoke good English. That made the decision for us. She told us that she would need £8,000 to take on the case, this being a fixed fee throughout Spain. It was a lot of money, but I knew Johnny had some money put aside from the sale of his house, which he had planned to use to start up a business. The thought of spending so much just to prove he was innocent was painful, but the money wouldn't do him any good if he were sent to a Moroccan prison for years. We were now beginning to fully realise that things could go badly wrong for Johnny if we didn't take some positive action. Inés was our only hope, the only straw we could clutch at. She agreed to go and see him.

Once she had been paid she went to work, trying to find out what was going on. It didn't take her long to unearth the story of what had happened to the boat after Johnny, Colin and the others left her in Agadir. I was vaguely aware of the story of the delivery of the *Cygnet*, but it was only one of the many stories John had told me in the eighteen months of our relationship, so I wasn't clear on any of the details. It had all been such a long time ago and seemed of little importance.

'It was a huge haul of cocaine,' she told us. 'One of the biggest ever – 6 tons. The seizure took place ten weeks after they delivered the boat, on the 20th of June 1997.'

The Moroccan authorities had issued international arrest warrants that year on all four British crew members. The charges were 'associating with drug traffickers and supplying equipment for the trafficking of narcotics' (ie the boat). Armed with this information I was able to locate numerous reports from 1997 on the internet and it was only then that the magnitude of the case began to be revealed.

It seemed the British government had unwittingly sold the *Cygnet* to the Cali Cartel, probably the biggest of the Colombian drug manufacturing, smuggling and distribution organisations. Some estimates suggested that the cartel controlled 80 per cent of cocaine exports from Colombia to the US. This was big-time organised crime.

The boat's name had been changed to the *Duanas* after Johnny and the others left Agadir. The cartel, who wanted to move the drugs from South America to Spain, planned to transfer them to the *Duanas* from another boat at sea, just off Las Palmas on the Canary Islands. They had ignored Johnny's advice to overhaul the engines and clean out the fuel tanks before setting out to sea again. The engines duly failed and the coastguards caught them drifting off the Moroccan coast, but not before the new crew had managed to dump a large proportion of their cargo overboard.

The packages washed up on the beaches, strewn along more than 75 miles of Moroccan shoreline – hundreds of them. Some people realised what they were and handed them to the police, many tried to sell them on and others, not realising what the white powder was, attempted to do their laundry with the stuff. It was reported at the time that ten-year sentences were being dished out to anyone found in possession. The Moroccan authorities were furious and wanted to ensure the Cali Cartel never operated in their country again. However, the only genuine names they could find any record of in connection with the boat were Johnny and his fellow crew members. Because they had been innocently delivering a boat they had used their own passports and had no reason to try to cover their tracks in any way, unlike the cartel members who used false ID for everything. British Interpol might have satisfied themselves that Johnny was innocent – not even bothering to interview the others – but the Moroccans were determined to find out the truth for themselves. For some political reason, heads had to roll and, years later,

Johnny's was the only one they could find. There was no way the British government would ever agree to extraditing a British citizen to Morocco, so it was incredibly bad luck that after seven years Johnny was arrested in Spain.

Knowing that the European courts were not inclined to try Johnny, the Moroccans wanted him extradited to their country to stand trial there. They wanted to make an example of someone and be seen to be fighting the war on drugs.

'Can they get away with that?' Catherine asked Inés.

'Spain has a reciprocal treaty with Morocco,' Inés explained, 'and they are obliged to extradite John if the request is made through the proper channels and seems reasonable.'

'So what happens next?'

'The Moroccan government has to file papers in Spain within thirty days, putting their case for the extradition to go ahead,' Inés went on. 'They probably won't get round to doing it. And it's hard to imagine how they could make a case that the Spanish would accept.'

'What if the paperwork hasn't arrived in thirty days?'

'Then John will be released. The Spanish have no reason to hold him if there is not going to be any extradition.'

'So whatever happens, John will be in prison for at least thirty days?'

'Yes, I believe so,' Inés said.

Thirty days sounded like an eternity, and very unfair when he hadn't done anything wrong, but at least it didn't sound as if he was going to have to go to Morocco, where prison conditions were likely to be a lot worse, not to mention their judicial system. What made it seem even more unfair was the discovery that the Spanish wouldn't be obliged to extradite one of their own nationals, only someone from another country. The treaty was probably set up to try to combat the trafficking of drugs and people between Northern Africa and Southern Europe, but no other country in Europe had an arrangement like this. Spain would eventually have to change this to fit in with European rules, but that was how the law stood at that moment and there was nothing we could do about it. Inés told us that she would be visiting John in prison to explain his situation to him. At least now we had an ally in the country, someone who knew their way around the system.

Every experienced prisoner Johnny spoke to would shake their heads and take a sharp intake of breath when he told them he was up for extradition. They all said he hadn't a hope of escaping it and that the whole process could take at least two years. He could fight it all the way but eventually everyone goes. They predicted he would be moved first to Madrid and that it would take days to get him there.

'You'll be cooped up in sweat boxes for days,' they warned, 'with a load of other criminals who are just as anxious and jumpy as you.'

'Don't listen to prison gossip,' Inés scolded him when he confided his fears to her. 'You'll be out in thirty days.'

We decided that since we had hired her, we had better put our faith in her and stay optimistic. If she thought Johnny would be out in thirty days, that was what we would work towards.

Back in England, the media had got wind of what was happening and started ringing and knocking on the door. Part of me was grateful and thought that publicity might be our way of getting the message across, but the other part of me was nervous about the invasion of my privacy. I also had Freya to think about. If Catherine and I opened the doors to the newspapers, who knew where it would all end? Eventually we reached a sort of compromise. When Meridian Television showed an interest we agreed to be filmed, and we talked to all the local newspapers. But when the *Daily Mirror* offered to run a campaign on our behalf we backed away, unwilling to get involved in the tabloid newspaper world, hoping that we would be able to get Johnny home without going to those extremes.

As the weeks passed we became more used to dealing with journalists, photographers and cameramen, and we started to lose some of the fear we had initially felt. The television seemed to be the best medium for us as we could appeal directly to the public and we had a better idea of how we would be portrayed. As we became more worried we started to feed them new angles every week to try to make sure that Johnny's name remained at the forefront of people's minds. One of my worst fears was that he would simply be forgotten, left to rot in a cell just because no one had got round to doing anything about it. At the same time I was worried that if we stirred up too much controversy in the media we might aggravate the Moroccan authorities even more and make them determined to prove that they were right and Johnny was guilty. On one day more our story appeared on six different news bulletins, but still it didn't seem to have any impact on Johnny's day-to-day routine in Spain. It felt like we were shouting into the wind.

CHAPTER THREE

John

Inés, the Spanish lawyer that Jane and Catherine had hired, came to visit me and explained that I was going to have to wait thirty days before the whole extradition thing was sorted out. While the thought of having to endure prison for a whole month was bad, it was a huge relief to find I had a lawyer who understood what was happening and was going to be watching over me. I no longer felt completely abandoned and alone.

'Then what will happen?' I asked.

'If sufficient paperwork linking you to this crime is not on the judge's desk in thirty days, then they will have to set you free,' she said, 'because they won't have any evidence against you. You are innocent, aren't you?'

'Yes,' I assured her.

'Then Spain will not be able to make a just case to send you. Keep calm and you'll be out by the 10th of November.'

The thought of thirty days of uncertainty mixed with tedium and fear was daunting, but I realised I wasn't being offered any options. I was just going to have to put it down as one of life's experiences. Having to pay the lawyer had made it a very expensive experience, but at that moment I was not as worried about the money as I was about the thought of being whisked away to a Moroccan prison cell.

After Inés' visit I discovered that Malaga was only a transit prison for me. They were just waiting to transfer me up to Valdemoro, a maximum security establishment on the plains outside Madrid, about 300 miles away from Malaga. But no one told me that. They didn't tell me anything, apart from 'do this' and 'go there'. I was living from moment to moment, unable to plan or anticipate what might be in store for me – a bit like a small child having his life arranged for him.

I didn't want to move. I wanted to stay in the cell I was used to, with the friendly Antonio. Prison is a frightening environment and once you have got used to your partic-ular little corner you don't want to be faced with any new, unknown factors. Every potential change holds fear. As the days had passed I had begun to become more used to my daily routines – the first signs of institutionalisation taking over, I guess. There were thin layers of foam on the bunks, which made them more comfortable than the ones in the first cell and I didn't want to lose them. There was also a table, a television and a little barred window giving a glimpse of blue sky. Antonio had been there long enough to get himself well set up. He even had his own snacks and let me share some of his Ryvita-style bread with cream cheese on top. He was a friendly man and happy for me to go on watching his television once he had gone to sleep. I found it hard to sleep with all the noise of the block, not that I understood a word of what was going on. Television helped to drown out the sound of the angry, aggressive voices of my real world. I hadn't even realised Billy Connolly made movies, and to see such a familiar face from my other life speaking in Spanish was surreal yet comforting in a strange way.

I had become hungry for any news about England, trying to leave the prison in my head if nothing else. I had never been much of a football fan, but I found myself glued to Liverpool playing a European match. Not everyone had televisions in their cells and some of the other Brits would have given up their visiting rights in exchange for the chance to watch such a big match. Most of the longer-term prisoners had access to television and would be avidly following any match, erupting simultaneously with joy or anger as the fortunes of their local teams ebbed and flowed. The eventual score that day was 0–0, reinforcing my doubts about the entertainment value of the game.

The other sport that united almost everyone in the prison, but which made me feel sick, was bull fighting. I loathed everything about it, but it was hard to avoid since it is as popular in Spain as football is in Britain. There were hundreds of fights a week. I hated the way such gorgeous animals were humiliated and tortured for the pleasure of the crowd, or the way they all cheered, laughed and applauded at the bulls' slow, agonising deaths. Why would anyone want to do that to any living creature for fun? Maybe it made my fellow inmates feel better to see something worse off than themselves, even if it was just an animal.

At night, when there wasn't anything on television, I would lie on the bunk, unable to sleep, looking up at the hundreds of dried bogeys that had stuck to the underside of Antonio's bed, wondering who they had belonged to, how long they had hung there and where their owner was now. Was he still in prison or was he free? Whatever, his bogeys were staying. Jokingly I wondered if perhaps I could pick them off and make something out of them, like some bizarre model a prisoner would build out of matchsticks. I hoped Antonio wouldn't move around too much up there or I would get covered.

In the mornings I would wake up with more flea bites on me than Badger, my dog. The blankets and mattresses must have been alive with them. I wondered if Badger was missing me as much as I was missing her. Would she still recognise me when I got back; or would she now have become Jane's dog while I was away? I felt so bad about having dumped all my problems on Jane – looking after Mum and Badger, worrying about money and sorting out my house and lodger – as if she didn't have enough to do already with her own home, her job and Freya to take care of. On top of all this, she and Catherine were spending hours each day trying to get me out of jail. It was so frustrating to have hours and hours every day with nothing to do and not to be able to do anything to help.

I started writing a lot about my feelings and thoughts and experiences, still convinced I would soon be out and on my way home. I had never had so much time to just sit and think about things. When you have that much time your imagination starts to take you to strange places. I remember watching a perfectly formed little black cloud drifting slowly across a perfect blue sky, thinking how wonderful it would be to be sitting on it, sailing across Europe and jumping off when I spotted the Isle of Wight. I could picture the whole scene as I knocked on Jane's front door. Badger would come bounding out, bouncing with excitement as always. The trouble with these flights of imagination was that I always had to come back down to earth at the end of them and remember where I was.

After another week I was told to pack my things so I could be taken back to *ingresso*, ready to be strip-searched again in the same routine as on arrival. It only took a couple of minutes to pack my towel, notebook, T-shirt, toilet roll and cigarettes, which were now my worldly possessions.

'Madrid?' I asked the prison guard as I was ushered into yet another cell in *ingresso*, remembering the predictions the other inmates had made.

'Tomorrow, Inglish, tomorrow,' he said, before slamming the door and leaving me alone. A big sodium searchlight flooded the cell with a bright orange glow through the window. I realised as I looked at the bare bunk that I was supposed to have brought my bedding in with me, but I had misunderstood and had packed it to go to Madrid with my other stuff. It meant I was going to have no bedding for the night, but it was stifling hot anyway so I wasn't too bothered.

The cell had seemed unusually clean as I walked in, and I soon realised why. Someone had been through all the holding cells with a power wash, something that certainly never happened on the wings. Everything was soaking wet, including the thin foam mattress. There was no chance of lying down.

Ingresso was always busy. New people were arriving every half hour, to the accompaniment of banging doors and shouts back and forth between the cell windows in a variety of languages – Arabic, Spanish, Portuguese – as people tried to find out who was arriving and what they were in for, searching for friends and contacts, or just information. As usual I stayed quiet as the hubbub went on around me. If there were any other Brits there, they too were keeping their own counsel. I didn't hear any English voices in the general commotion.

EXTRADITED!

Tired, hot and humiliated by the strip-search, I no longer felt like a human being. I could almost feel myself turning into an animal as the days went past, like so many of the other men I was now living with. I already smelled as strongly as them and most of my time was spent thinking how to get something else to eat or drink or smoke, or some small luxury to make life more comfortable or to distract me for a few minutes from the endless cocktail of boredom and anxiety. When personal survival is your only real goal each day, you aren't much more than an animal.

The next morning, after an uncomfortable night sitting on a plastic stool due to the wet mattress, I was given a cold coffee and a hard roll, handcuffed and thrown into the back of a police van. I was soon to get used to these vehicles, converted coaches known as 'sweat boxes'. They were filled with about a dozen tiny compartments the size of Portaloos, just big enough for two men to sit side by side, cuffed together, having to rub arms and shoulders in the sweltering heat. The smell of urine was overpowering, the walls covered in grime, gob and snot. It was impossible not to rub up against them as the vehicle lurched forward, sending you off balance. There was no ventilation or natural light and the sweat dripped off me from the moment we sat down.

Luckily my fellow traveller was a Brit and he told me his name was Bobby. For what seemed the hundredth time that week I told him my story. In return he told me he was doing three years for causing a car accident when he was drunk. I had already learned that it was impossible to tell who was telling the truth and who was exaggerating their stories to impress their listeners, or maybe just to amuse themselves, but it didn't matter any more. I wasn't interested in the truth or otherwise about my fellow inmates, just having a distraction from my own thoughts and some communication with another person was enough.

Even though I had only just met Bobby I was beginning to like him. We talked about our lives, even found some things in common. We discovered we had both travelled to Israel. As we talked he shared his cheese roll with me, even though I had been given one myself. It was one of the few examples of camaraderie I'd experienced since my arrest – someone giving me something without wanting anything in return. We talked non-stop, about places we'd travelled to and the many things we'd seen. It was the first proper conversation I'd had since getting on my plane at Gatwick, which seemed like an age away.

After four hours of swaying and sweating in the box, we arrived at our destination. Taking deep lungfuls of fresh cool air again, we were herded into the new *ingresso* to be strip-searched once again, finger printed and photographed in the now familiar routine. It took nearly half a day just to get twelve people processed. They let me take cigarettes, a bottle of water, a toothbrush, a towel and a plastic mug from my black bin liner. Then Bobby and I were escorted to our holding cell, where a previous occupant had scrawled the words 'Welcome to Hell' in English on the walls.

'Are we in Madrid?' I asked Bobby.

'I dunno,' he shrugged. It didn't matter where we were really, we were still in prison.

I decided to eat a scabby apple that I'd been hanging onto for three days, waiting for a special moment. After a few hours we were moved into a tiny courtyard, about half the size I was used to. I watched two sparrows coming and going from a nest they had built in a crack in the wall. It seemed ironic that they should choose to share our prison space when they had the freedom to go anywhere. Dinner was a poor excuse for a pork chop – thin, hard and dry – along with chips, all cold.

When they banged us up for the night the bright lights stayed on and we realised they had no intention of turning them off as they wanted to keep an eye on us. It was too bright to sleep so Bobby and I worked out that we could smash the bulb if we poked a pen through the protective grill. A few sharp jabs and it shattered, allowing a soothing darkness to fall. Now all we had to keep us awake were the fleas and mosquitoes, the sounds of slamming doors and the smells.

The next morning we discovered that we weren't anywhere near Madrid. We had only reached the first staging post of our journey north. As we strolled around the courtyard our names were being called out, one by one. When mine was called I realised we were yet again on the move. I had to kick up a fuss because I had left my trusty jacket up in the cell. The guard finally allowed me to rush up. As I closed the door behind me I took a last look. There were Bobby's bits and pieces all neatly laid out. Goodbye Bobby, I said to myself. I liked him a lot. He'd shown me kindness, which was rare in prison. He didn't need to be nice. Cuffed to new strangers, I was sad to be parted from him. When you meet someone you get on with in prison you don't want to lose them, but we were obviously heading in different directions.

The next night I repeated the whole process at another prison, although I was given better food this time, including a pear and a yoghurt, and a cell by myself. Such small improvements make the most extraordinary difference to your morale when you are at that low an ebb. Standing at the window, watching the sunset and savouring the pear, trying to make it last, I wondered how I could ever have got myself into this position. The door opened and my metal dinner tray was picked up by another prisoner.

'You English?' he asked.

'Yes,' I replied.

He handed me four cigarettes. It was a small gesture of kindness but it meant a great deal, not only because I had run out, but because it showed that not everyone was an asshole. I went back to the window as the darkness fell and watched the bats circling round the searchlight outside. It was a long night, alone in that cell. Sharing a cell is horrible but it keeps you on your toes and makes the time pass quicker. The next day, when I was loaded back into the van once again, I found myself cuffed to a guy who informed me he'd been in the cell next to mine. He told me he was the one who had sent the cigarettes via the man collecting the trays; he was my anonymous benefactor.

'I felt sorry for you,' he said, 'on your own all night.'

I thanked him for the thought, but at the back of my mind I wondered what he was going to want in exchange. Just being in prison for that short a time had taught me that hardly anyone inside does anything for nothing. It made it hard to accept a spontaneous gesture of kindness for what it was. The following night the whole *ingresso* ritual was repeated again at yet another holding prison. Only on the fourth night did I finally reach Valdemoro, my destination, and went through the *ingresso* procedure for the fifth time in as many days. I was getting so used to it I no longer had to be told what to do during the strip-searches, just followed the routine. I was turning into an old hand.

All the way up to Madrid the driver and guards had set their own itinerary as they went, without any thought to what effect it would have on us in our sweat boxes. If they fancied stopping for a meal or a siesta they would do so, leaving the van with us in it, cooking in the sun for hours on end. As we sat, sweating in our little boxes, we had no idea what was happening outside or how long it would be before we were on our way again. We were just cargo to be moved from one place to another.

At Valdemoro I found myself in a holding cell with fifteen other prisoners. They looked like hardened criminals, heavily tattooed and scarred, and none of them spoke English. Some of them shouted through the bars at the screws to come and move us on. Everyone was hot and restless, but the guards had gone for their siestas again. If something went wrong for me in this cell there was no one to come to my rescue. I felt like I was travelling further and further from my known world. At least there had been some prisoners I could communicate with in Malaga; now I was isolated by my native language.

I sat in the corner and kept my eyes on the floor, not wanting to aggravate anyone by staring at them. This was a maximum security prison, full of the country's most ruthless criminals, and I didn't want any trouble. So I just waited to find out what was going to happen to me next. Valdemoro had a dozen or more wings and a total of 1,700 prisoners; another batch of newcomers were an insignificant part of their daily routine. I had no idea what lay in store for me next.

Jane

My whole time seemed to be spent trying to communicate with Johnny, which for a while proved impossible as he was in transit from Malaga to Madrid. Even the embassy was unsure of his whereabouts.

Once he was in Valdemoro he was allowed a five-minute call five days a week, but if he rang and I wasn't there he didn't get another chance until the next day. I would always rush to be home at the times when he was likely to call and all my friends and family knew not to call me during those hours. Not having a regular time that Johnny would call kept me in a permanent state of anxiety.

I always kept a list of things I had to talk to him about, constantly reassuring him we were doing everything possible to get him back home. But Johnny would have a list too – full of his thoughts and ideas that he'd come up with during the hours with nothing to do but sit and think about his situation, or questions and worries inspired by conversations with other prisoners.

Both of us would be desperate to get through our lists before the phone call ran out, so we would end up trying to shout over one another in our rush. We never seemed to get a chance to relax and have a normal day-to-day conversation, like saying how much we missed one another. Johnny would want to ask after Freya or his mum or Badger, but we had to talk about lawyers and extradition laws and money all the time. Sometimes I had to find out really mundane stuff, like how to get the central heating going in his house. Important phone minutes would be used up on how to keep Johnny's life in order at home. However, I would always try to find something positive and uplifting for the end of each call.

'I was talking to a guy here,' Johnny said, during his first week in Madrid, 'a Croatian, an old guy with all this long grey hair. He says I'll definitely have to go to Morocco. Everyone they try to extradite gets sent in the end. He says the whole process could take a year.'

'Do you think he's right?' I asked, horrified at the thought.

'No,' he laughed, a little uncertainly, 'I told him, I'm innocent, I'm just a normal working man. They won't put me through all that. He didn't believe me. Everyone in these places is an expert!'

I hung up that day with a heavy heart. What would happen to Johnny if the Moroccans managed to get him extradited? How would we be able to help him to fight the charges when he was so far away? How would he survive in a Moroccan jail during these troubled times in the Middle East? How would he hold up mentally if the whole process really took a year to go through? It didn't seem possible that an innocent man could be deprived of a year or two of his life before he had even been charged with a crime.

I forced all these thoughts to the back of my mind, reminding myself that Inés had been sure he would be released after thirty days. I had to believe she was right, just to hold on to my own sanity.

John

Eventually the guards came back, to a cheer from the waiting prisoners, and switched their computers back on. One by one our names would be called out and the barred gates of the holding cell would open up automatically to allow us out. We would be strip-searched again and have our photographs taken. Then we would be given our bedrolls.

As the crowd in the cell thinned out I became particularly aware of a big, menacing-looking man with short bleached-blonde hair and thickly muscled arms bulging out of his over-tight orange T-shirt. He was about 6 foot 3 inches and built like the Incredible Hulk; if I could have chosen him as a fighter in a PlayStation 2 game, I would have. He looked like a nightclub bouncer and he was gabbling in Spanish to the others left in the holding cell, entertaining them and seeming to be having a great laugh. It was obvious that everyone was a little wary of him, humouring him. He seemed a bit of a prat to me, but I didn't take too much notice, wanting to keep myself to myself, staring at the floor to avoid any eye contact with anyone.

One by one the others were called out. About four hours after we had first been put into the cell there was only me, one other guy and the blonde man left. I knew it was my turn next to be the focus of his attention and I felt a shiver of dread. Sure enough he started talking to me.

'Me no understand,' I said, trying to look as unthreatening and uninteresting as possible. 'I'm English.'

'Oh,' he said with a broad grin, 'fucking English are you, mate?'

It turned out he was from Moss Side in Manchester and his name was Jim.

'Where're you from?' he asked.

'Down south,' I said, my mouth dry and my throat clogged, having not spoken to anyone for hours.

He barged the other man aside and sat down next to me. He seemed to have no fear or inhibitions at all.

'I've been inside for two years,' he said, passing me a cigarette. 'Haven't spoken English for months. How are yer doing, man?'

To my relief it felt as if he liked me. I was sitting with someone who thought he was 'the Daddy' and it occurred to me that if I befriended him he just might offer me some protection in the world I was about to enter. I accepted the cigarette and asked him about himself.

He told me he owned a nightclub in Tenerife, although I suspected he just worked there.

'You stay by me, mate, you'll be fine.'

We talked all night about his flash car, flash nightclub, and how he watched his mum die in his arms from cancer when he was ten. He told me all about his life of crime; apparently he was a big drug dealer on Moss Side, leading a life filled with guns and shoot-outs. I had no way of telling how much of it was true, but I liked him because he seemed to like me. He told me he was wanted for extradition as well, for a double murder.

'But it wasn't "just any old murder",' he confided. 'It was an execution. Wearing the old ballys [balaclavas] and taking them out into the woods, getting them on their knees with the guns at the backs of their heads, screaming for their lives as I popped two caps into their fucking heads. I was paid a hundred grand each so I went to Tenerife and bought the nightclub.'

The club was subsequently raided for drugs and in the course of the raid they found credit card making machines, which was what he was in prison for. He was looking at six years in Spain for that before he could be extradited back to Britain to stand trial for the double murder. Apparently they had caught up with him because they had found one of the balaclavas and it had his DNA all over it. I had no way of judging how likely this all was to be true, but he certainly told it convincingly.

Eventually it was our turn to be called out to be searched and to collect our belongings. You could tell which prisoners had been inside the longest by the amount of possessions they had managed to collect. I was still travelling very light.

'Don't worry, bro,' he said when he saw a look of consternation pass over my face. 'You're with me now. I won't let anyone hurt you. I'll fuckin' kill them first.'

I wasn't sure what I had let myself in for, but I didn't think I had much choice as he was the only person I'd met, apart from Bobby, who spoke English. Our next stop was the medical centre and he stepped in as my interpreter, looming over the obviously intimidated doctor. He was talking about me in Spanish and I had no way of knowing how to react. Only later did I discover what he had been saying.

'He can't sleep,' he told the doctor. 'His brain just doesn't switch off when the lights go out.'

That resulted in me being given a week's supply of sleeping pills and being told to come back for stronger ones if they didn't work. Jim relieved me of the tablets immediately, knowing he could use them to trade with on the wing.

'They're good,' he said approvingly when I handed them over, 'but nothing like as good as what I've got. I'll give you some later, bro.'

When we were moved to the main wing the next day we were split up into separate cells, despite Jim's best bullying tactics to try to keep us together. My new cell-mate was a Spaniard called Royale.

'Hi,' I said as I stepped into the cell for the first time, pointing to myself. 'John.'

I held out my hand but he brushed it aside, uninterested in talking to me or having anything else to do with me. I tried offering him biscuits and sweets over the following days, like one might to an unfriendly dog, but he ignored me every time. It was clear he had no interest in me at all. If looks could have killed I would not have woken up the following morning. At 9.30 pm he turned the lights out without a word and we lay in silence in the darkness together, waiting for sleep to arrive. Things between us never improved from there. Time dragged slowly and I felt totally alienated, knowing this cell-mate did not want me in there with him.

Two days later I was moved into a cell with an Argentinian guy known as 'The Doc', who had smuggled a ton of cocaine into Spain on his own boat. He was sixty-two years old and he was going to be in there for at least ten years. He actually was a trained doctor who had been trying to make a fast buck so he could live out his days in luxury, and now he was set to spend the rest of them in prison. It turned out Doc had asked a guard if I could be moved in with him, so he didn't end up with someone less desirable than me. I was happy with the move if only for the conversation and advice on prison life. He was a nice old man, broken but still keen to help others. I stayed with him for a week before he asked to have me moved out. His excuse was a friend was coming onto the wing and he wanted him to replace me. It was a shame but I wasn't going to miss his snoring.

Next was Carlos, a young Italian who seemed to like me despite the language barrier. His father lived in Spain and he had a wife and kids living in Germany. He had come to visit his father for the weekend. The house was raided for something his father had done and Carlos was arrested at the same time. He hadn't known anything about what his father had been up to. He could still wait up to two years before knowing his fate. We communicated through sign language and played chess most nights for two weeks, until another Italian arrived and he wanted me out as well. Once again, I found myself searching for a suitable cell-mate, someone I could cope with when locked together in a small room for sixteen out of twenty-four hours. I wondered if I was always going to be moving from pillar to post.

There was no choice left but to move in with Jim. He was very friendly and seemed keen to look out for me on my first days in the jail. Although he was a bit frightening it was a relief to find someone twice my size who was offering to take me under his wing and show me the ropes as we were being processed. He had kept asking the screws to allow us to share a cell, and his request had finally been granted. Because I was hanging out with him during the day, and because he looked pretty scary, I wasn't getting too many problems from anyone else, although I was paying 20 euros a week in protection money to some other tough guys who were promising to beat me up if I didn't. I wasn't too worried about moving in with Jim, thinking he would sort me out with these guys and at least I would have someone to talk to. He had started to pick on me a bit during the day, as if I was getting on his nerves, and I hoped that if we shared a cell he might feel an obligation to start looking after me again.

I had seen a good few fights within my first few days and I had confided to Jim that I didn't like the idea of that. There was a group of Romanians who were particularly violent about getting money off other inmates.

'I've come in here with a good set of teeth,' I explained to Jim, 'and I'd like to go home with them.'

'I'll look after yer,' he assured me at the time.

I had a bit of money, which Jane had sent through to my prison account, so I was able to return his kindness to me with cigarettes. I was allowed £50 a week spending money for things like drinks, cigarettes, sweets, proper soap, stationery and razors. After a while Jim didn't even bother asking for a cigarette, just held his hand out and expected to be given one. It was as if he had trained me to be his lackey through a mixture of intimidation and protection. To begin with it was easier to just go along with it, but gradually I realised he was now exploiting me more than the people he was protecting me from would. He had been using my money to buy cannabis, telling me it would be sold on and my money returned. But of course he smoked it and used it to make friends.

I also had a bit of extra money, about £100, which I'd managed to smuggle in with me when I was moved from Malaga. I was supposed to hand it in in *ingresso*, but I was able to smuggle two £50 notes onto the wing, hidden in the lining of my jacket. Being under the impression that I would be going home soon, I thought it would be handy to have some money to pay for a ticket as soon as I was released. I then got cold feet and thought about handing it in to the guards, in case it was found during one of many cell searches, or 'spins' as they were called. I asked Jim's advice and he was adamant I should hold onto it.

'Don't give it in, mate,' he urged me. 'You're going to need that in here.'

It wasn't long before I realised why. Having used up my weekly allowance he asked me to hand over my secret stash. I didn't want to hand it over because the protection payments were eating into my cash and I needed it to buy myself enough food to survive – no one could survive on prison rations alone. Most dinners would consist of fish-head soup and a hard bread roll. I'd noticed that whenever I got to the bottom of my bowl there would always be far more eyes looking at me than tallied up with the heads.

I realised that I had to stand up to him this time, or I would end up having everything taken off me. I refused to hand over the money, my heart thumping uncomfortably in my chest. Furious to discover that he hadn't completely subjugated me and that I had dared to say no to him, he started bullying me on a daily basis, pinning me up against the wall and threatening to knock my teeth out if I didn't hand over the money. He was completely successful at frightening the life out of me, but I knew I couldn't give in or I would be within his power for ever.

Sharing a cell with him was a big mistake. He had decided to make my life a misery and he wasn't going to change his mind now just because we were cell-mates. One night he decided to pull me off the top bunk by my arm, for fun. I knew if I hit my head on the edge of the concrete table on the way to the floor it would kill me, but he just thought it was a great laugh – a typical playground bully. After two nights of hell I asked to be moved and the guards obliged, obviously knowing why because they didn't ask me for any reasons. They must have been watching all his activities through the darkened glass windows of their office, because it wasn't long before he was removed from the wing altogether and I was left to deal only with the Romanians.

They put me in a cell with a German who had no English but seemed to be a nice enough criminal, just like Carlos. We made up a set of dominoes using the card from an empty tissue box, anything to pass the hours of boredom. He liked me even more when I offered him some puff, which I had realised was the best way to make myself fit in. It wasn't hard to find someone who would be willing to sell you any sort of drugs you wanted, and could afford. I tried hash, thinking it might provide a distraction from my worries and would dull the boredom a bit, but it didn't. It just made my mind do even crazier things and worry even more about what would happen if I was never able to get out. The paranoia was so overwhelming I stopped.

Although the guards always seemed to know what was going on among the prisoners, they didn't take any notice because they rarely came onto the wing. They just watched everything that went on through one-way, bulletproof glass windows, which were heavily barred. You knew they were behind the glass because now and then you would see a light going on or off and a shadow moving, but all the doors on the wing were activated by remote control when they wanted to herd us from one area to another, so they seldom had to actually come out among us. Most of the time it was like being watched and controlled by an unseen 'Big Brother'. One day a prisoner had an epileptic fit in the dining room and swallowed his tongue. He'd gone blue and stopped breathing and a few of the other inmates were trying to help him, but none of the screws appeared, even though they must have been able to see what was happening on camera. They must have made a phone call from behind their glass barriers because a couple of inmates from another wing arrived through remote-controlled doors with a stretcher to take him to the hospital wing. It was almost like the whole wing was being operated by remote control.

Every morning we would be woken at 7.30 am with a loud bang on the door. We had to turn our lights on and give the guard a wave through the peephole, to show we were still there and hadn't topped ourselves or killed one another in the night. I would try to get back to sleep for half an hour but my brain would be awake by then, reminding me of where I was and that I had another long, empty day stretching ahead of me. I would toss and turn on my lumpy mattress, recalling memories of the Isle of Wight, longing so much to be back there that it was almost a physical pain. Eventually I would get up, wash and dress. At 8.00 am, if there had been no overnight dramas, such as a suicide (it was not good to have inmates wandering around and seeing someone hanging), the doors would be unlocked and we would come down from our cells, walking through dimly lit corridors, and start queuing. If you weren't ready to leave when the door opened you would be in trouble.

'Trouble' could mean being banged up for fifteen days, locked in a cell, only being allowed down for meals and no privileges such as phone calls or visits to the prison shop. Three small crimes, like not being ready to come out of your cell on time, or one big thing like swearing at a screw, would get you 'trouble'. Fighting, having drugs or a mobile phone would get you sent off the wing to 'the block', where you could end up spending as much as three months in solitary confinement.

The cells were on two floors and they would alternate which floor they would open first each morning, to give us all a fairer chance of getting to the front of the queues which governed our lives.

Our cell doors would be locked behind us so we couldn't go back in until they allowed us to. Once you were out there was no hiding place – from the cameras of the screws or the eyes of your fellow inmates. To get back to your cell you had to be either seriously ill or kicking off and about to be punished. Every time one of these movements to or from the cells took place there would be the repetitive sound of keys turning in locks and doors slamming, over and over again. I did the maths and worked out that each officer must turn their keys 600 times a day. Each opening or closing process could take as long as half an hour. The screws always seemed to love slamming doors behind us, leaving the noise ringing in our ears for minutes after they had gone. It must have been a way to release their own frustrations at the tedium of the job. They always wore latex gloves when they were on the wings, which made me wonder what sort of dangers they thought lurked in the filth we lived among. If they were worried about being exposed to germs, what were we being exposed to? Everything was dirty. If I was sitting on a chair I would never want to touch any part that hadn't been rubbed clean by thousands of backsides moving up and down. The sides would be thick with years of grime that you could peel off with your nail if you could face it.

The sounds of keys and doors were not only coming from our own wing, but echoing across the courtyards from the other wings as well. There was a constant, repetitive, echoing noise and never any peace or tranquillity.

We would be filtered downstairs from the cells through a series of automatic doors. We would queue for the coffee, queue for the toilets, queue to book our telephone calls for that day, queue for our breakfast; 180 men crushed together in a small area, pushing and shoving, waiting for things to happen, for time to pass, for their turn to come.

Choosing the right queues was an art form, having to decide which one held the best chance of you reaching the end. First I would check out the phone queue, then coffee, then toilets. I was often busting for the toilet due to my anxiety not to break the number one rule of 'don't shit in the cell'. Sometimes people would join a queue even though they didn't want whatever was at the end of it, knowing they would be able to sell their place for a cigarette or some other luxury once they got near the front. Queuing isn't a big problem when you have nothing else to do all day, but there were added complications, like not enough spaces on the telephone call sheets for all the inmates, which would lead to fights, everyone pushing, kicking and punching their way to the front, or taking a bite out of each other's ears in what often looked like explosions of sheer spite or boredom. Many of the successful ones would later barter their call times in exchange for cigarettes.

We all then had to squeeze through one small door for coffee, pushing against the people already coming out, like an overcrowded nightclub filled with stinking, unwashed men with greasy hair. If my bare arm rubbed up against someone else's, I could feel the sweat, slippery against my own skin, making me feel contaminated and dirty with no way of cleaning myself. The coffee would always run out as well before everyone had got to the front of the queue.

There would be another struggle to get in through the narrow door to the dining room as those who had already eaten struggled to get out and queue for the toilets. The prisoners working behind the counter in the dining area would suffer a lot of abuse, being seen as working for the screws. Other prisoners would spit at the glass that guarded them. The bread rolls they handed out were so hard I was nervous about biting into them. Having lost a gold cap from one of my teeth I was terrified of doing more damage and ending up with a serious toothache. The thought of having to visit a prison dentist was a terrifying prospect, particularly as I was informed he only did extractions. It felt like a trip back to the middle ages.

When we were booking our phone calls we would have to write down who we wanted to call and when we wanted to make the call. I would always book it between 5.45 pm and 6.15 pm, knowing that was the time I was most likely to catch Jane at home. I tried to keep to an agreed time, knowing poor Jane was stuck at home waiting for a call that might never come. Because I couldn't say the times in Spanish I would have to lean into the windows and point at the chart, which always angered the guards, who felt I was invading their space and being disrespectful, although some of them were beginning to get used to me. When my allotted time came round I would have to go and stand by the phone and hassle whoever was using it to try to get them to finish their call and let me make mine. No one ever took kindly to being asked to hand over the phone. It usually ended with an argument and sometimes I would lose two of my valuable minutes just trying to get the handset off the man in front.

On the upside, I would sometimes get extra time because the guy scheduled to come after me would be willing to sell his time for a packet of cigarettes, although the guards would become angry if they realised I'd done that – seeing it as cheating the system and taking more than my fair share. I was warned by other prisoners that if they caught me three times I could be banned from using the phone for anything up to six months, but I took my chances as I was desperate to hear a familiar voice. I had to be very careful to negotiate my extra time out of their sight and hearing. There were other Brits or prisoners who spoke English coming and going from the prison, some of whom were old hands and would fill me in on the rules and etiquette of prison life and how to get around them. I was aware though that not all advice was given for my benefit.

Sometimes the guards seemed to do things to annoy us on purpose, winding us up just to see us kick off. They would sometimes tell me I'd had all my five allotted calls for the week, when I knew I'd only had four because I logged everything down meticulously. I would try to argue my case but I knew at times I had to give in – if you became known as a troublemaker you could be moved out to a far worse wing, somewhere where the screws never intervened at all and the laws of the jungle were all that existed to protect the more vulnerable prisoners like me.

One night, just as I was being banged up, the guard told me to be ready for 7.00 am because I was going to be appearing in court the next day. I was sure I wasn't due for court and I began to panic, worried that Inés was 300 miles away in Malaga and knew nothing about what was going on. What if everything went wrong and I was whisked away to Morocco before she even found out it was happening? I had no way of contacting her, no way of getting access to a phone, no way of making any of the screws understand why I was worried.

The next morning, after a very anxious, sleepless night, I was loaded into a van with several other guys. I was wearing my nicest clothes, having court in mind. No one gave us any explanation as to what was going on. We were taken to a police station and put into a freezing cold underground holding cell where they left us without a word. Towards the end of the day I was hauled out, had a number put round my neck, and was shunted into a police line-up. That was all we were wanted for. We were there all day, without any food or drink, until they took us back to prison in the evening. I was so angry at being used for a police investigation without my consent.

The worst thing about prison is the boredom; every day is the same. I guess that's why some prisoners kick off the way they do, just to make something happen, anything. I had always been someone who needed to be busy. I had never been able to sit still for long, but now I had no alternative. We had to be out of our cells by 8.00 am and then, once the morning queues were over, the only thing to do was sit at a table, staring into space, or walk about the courtyard, smoking, trying to avoid bumping into people or even making eye contact. Sometimes a few men would get together a game of football, or would work out with some weights they built with water bottles strapped together, or run around punching the air like boxers in training. Others would take up children's hobbies like sticking bits of coloured cotton onto sticky-backed paper in order to create pictures, which looked even funnier than the air punchers – rapists, mass murderers, even ETA terrorists, heavy-set men covered in scars and tattoos doing embroidery.

There were half a dozen ETA terrorists on the wing, and the guards would keep shifting them from cell to cell so no one knew their exact whereabouts. One afternoon we were out in the courtyard when we heard a tremendous noise coming over the walls: shouting and cheering and the blasting of blow horns. They quickly banged us all up in the cells and we were able to see outside where about thirty people were blocking the road, waving banners and ETA flags. The terrorists on the wing were waving their little home-made flags out the windows like it was some kind of celebration and every other prisoner seemed to be shouting and cheering their support. The guards didn't let us out of the cells again that afternoon. We had 'lock down' for the rest of the day.

I saw several strong men cracking up under the strain. There was one in particular, a German businessman who was fine when he first came in and spoke pretty good English. I think he was in for a tax fraud of some sort. A couple of days later he started shaking and walking about in a repetitive fashion, up and down in front of the screws' office. He had a plastic bag of his belongings, which he carried with him everywhere, as if terrified of being parted from it. Two days later he was rubbing himself down the wall in one direction, then turning and doing the same in reverse, while constantly mumbling to himself. Only then did the guards come in and take him away. We never saw him again and it was rumoured he had gone for the electric shock treatment. Reports came back that he had been seen on the hospital wing, motionless, just staring into space. There were always rumours and prison tales circulating, because we all had so much time on our hands. I could completely understand how easily a man like that could be tipped over the edge by suddenly finding everything in his life reversed. From being someone who was probably in charge of every aspect of his life, he had suddenly been turned into an anonymous number, with no power to influence anything that happened to him.

There was also a Frenchman called José who had been in and out of prison quite a bit and used to go to the doctor for a shot of something twice a day. Whenever he came back down to the wing he would just be staring into space for hours, unable to focus on anything going on around him. I was terrified that if I didn't hold onto my self-control I could end up in the same state. One of the hardest things to cope with was the anxiety and not knowing what was happening. It would have been quite pleasant to have been able to escape from the worry with a dose of medication.

It was like being trapped on an endless cross-channel ferry trip, day after day, or in a dentist's waiting room or going round and round on a never-ending roundabout, where nothing ever changed in the routine. If you got into trouble and were sent 'down the block', it meant solitary confinement and a paper suit, no furniture, no books or magazines. At least having other people around gave you something to look at. I found a corner of the courtyard, underneath the 30-foot walls, where there was a bit of shade from the sun during the morning and I would sometimes take my blanket out and sit there until the sun came round and chased me back inside. For hours on end we would stand with our backs to walls, one knee bent, our boots adding to the black grime of the paintwork, just watching and waiting for the hours and days to pass. After a while your brain goes numb. I could imagine how hard it was for long-term prisoners to readjust once they were released back into the normal world and prayed I would never become one of them.

I would spend most of my time in the non-smoking room, because the air in the smoking area was too thick to bear, and the noise level was overwhelming. A lot of the inmates would play dominoes, banging them down on the tables with all their strength, shouting at the tops of their voices and arguing with one another just for the sake of it. The non-smoking room was usually quieter, with people reading, writing letters or making their tap-estries. It was a bit like being in the lounge of an old-folks home without the comfortable chairs. Sometimes a bunch of Romanians would come in and start larking about like adolescents, throwing tea and coffee over one another and generally showing off. There were cameras everywhere and if things got too rowdy the tannoy would crackle into life, spout some angry Spanish, and the perpetrators would move out of the room again.

Not speaking the language was an added problem, meaning that I couldn't understand most of what was going on around me. Everything that happened seemed to involve filling out a form in Spanish and I would have to find a friendly bilingual prisoner to help me with even the simplest things, like filling out my first visit forms. A Swiss guy called Pieter was a huge support to me in the early days. I owe him so much for the hours he spent each day talking reason to me. He was a wealthy man who was inside for some white-collar crime and would often help out other prisoners with money so they could hire half-decent lawyers rather than having to rely on the local ones. He and I struck up a friendship and would always sit together at the same table in the non-smoking room. Pieter could see that sometimes I was scared. He could see the fear on my face if a situation got out of hand or if bad news arrived from home. He was one of the few who believed I was innocent.

When anyone else from the table left the prison we would quickly choose someone else we liked the look of and ask them if they'd like to join us, in an attempt to keep ourselves apart from the nastier people on the wing. There were some nice people in there, even if some of them had committed hideous crimes; you just had to seek them out. There was an American guy who sat with us for a while who was awaiting extradition. He was accused of killing eight women, but he was always very pleasant company. There was no way of knowing if he was guilty of the crimes or not but just listening to some of his stories told me he was capable of anything. Pieter on the other hand was different. I knew he was a kind man.

Pieter was good at lifting my spirits whenever things looked particularly hopeless. I usually knew he was bullshitting, but it was still good to hear someone being optimistic, assuring me that everything would work out all right.

'There are plenty of things we can do to get you out,' he would say. 'There's nothing to worry about.'

But we both knew there was. If there had been nothing to worry about I would have been out and home already. Something was going wrong behind the scenes, but I had no way of getting to the bottom of what it might be, and my imagination fed me an endless stream of possible outcomes to my predicament, none of them good.

I learnt to ration whatever entertainment I had. If Jane had sent me a newspaper, I would read it for ten minutes and then go for a walk around the courtyard, read for another ten minutes and then take a cigarette break. A sudoku puzzle or a crossword could be eked out for hours. That way I could make one newspaper last all day. I would spend hours just reading all the ads once I'd finished with the editorial. I knew everything there was to know about mobile phone deals.

There seemed to be so much bad news in the papers, but it was strangely and sadly comforting to know that I wasn't the only one having a terrible time, and if I read about something like a brutal murder I could tell myself I was lucky to be where I was, desperately scrabbling around to find blessings to count.

I learnt early on that it was not good to think too much about my situation. The best plan was to shut my brain down for as long as possible each day. Everyone in there did the same – it was the only way to stay sane. When I did think about it I would feel guilty for all the pressure I knew I was putting on Jane, who was having to do all my thinking for me. We both knew that if she didn't act I would be in prison a lot longer, my case lost in the backlog of paperwork.

Newspapers and magazines were like gold dust, and it didn't matter how old they were, or even what language they were in. As soon as people saw I had a magazine they would start pestering to read it, or just to look at the pictures. In the end I would give in to the hassling and hand it over, just to have a quiet life. Everyone was starving for any sort of mental stimulation they could find, even if it was a two-week-old copy of the *Daily Mail* and they didn't speak English. I didn't get hassled so much if I was reading a book, because not enough people could read English and there weren't any pictures for them to look at. It was very rare to find an English book floating around.

In the afternoons we would all be banged up in our cells again, in the hottest part of the day. The windows were too small to let enough air in and the concrete walls seemed to glow like ovens with heat they had stored from the sun. I saw people holding bits of card out through the windows and realised they were trying to scoop in fresh air, catching any passing breeze and filtering cooler air into the cells, since we were not allowed electric fans. I thought I could do better than that and devised a method of tying the bits of cardboard through the bars at right angles to the windows with bootlaces, and reinforcing them so they didn't flap about too much. It worked particularly well at night. Just to be creative for a few hours was a relief. It gave me the chance to exercise my brain, giving myself a distraction and achieving a result. When you are being creative you are taking control of something. The agony of prison life is the lack of control over your own destiny.

Within a few days I noticed that everyone was tying up cardboard in the same way and there were lines and lines of it sticking out from every window. After a few weeks the authorities put a stop to it, swooping round the cells while we were out and collecting up the card. A sign went up saying we were forbidden to start again, and water to the cells was turned off for a day.

We were allowed to buy some extras from the prison shop, like extension leads and reading lamps. I became very excited the first time I had saved enough credit and could afford a little lamp which clipped under my bunk, so I could go on reading once the lights were out in the cells. Others went mad and got several leads and had lamps all round the cells, but the screws would confiscate them every so often in their swoops if you had more than the allocated amount. Others even had stereos but I was told I hadn't been there long enough to qualify for that. I longed for a radio so I could pass the hours listening to the World Service.

There was always noise going on when everyone was locked up – shouting, banging, singing, music. There was a lot of Moroccan music, which was a constant reminder of why I was there and what might lie in store for me. Anyone who agreed to be extradited would be gone within a couple of weeks and replaced by a new face. Some days I wondered if I should just agree to go and get the whole ordeal over with, but then a terrible fear of the unknown would return and I'd go back to reassuring myself that a way out could be found. Surely they wouldn't send a European to a place like Morocco?

Some of the prisoners, particularly those who needed to earn some pocket money, would take jobs as cleaners or would work in the canteen. We were all responsible for our own cells, but everywhere else prisoners were paid to keep the jail clean. After meals they would go round wiping the floors and tables with the same grubby mops. This was much better than not being cleaned at all, which often seemed to be the case in the toilets and showers.

The toilets were just stainless steel pans, which you had to queue up for, usually waiting at least twenty minutes. I would never sit down on them, and nor would the Arabs, preferring to stand in the traditional manner, as I realised when I saw footprints on the rims of the toilet bowls. They didn't bother with paper either, taking a bottle of water in with them instead. When you got behind the partitions, which was the closest we ever got to having any privacy, you found your face inches away from other people's dried spittle, often flecked with blood, your feet amidst piles of fag ends in puddles of piss, staring at the results of fellow prisoners' daily masturbations. They did at least provide little swing doors to the cubicles in Madrid, where the ones in Malaga had none, but there were only a few of them and the unbearable stench was the same. I would try to finish my business as quickly as possible and then burst back out into the main area, gasping for breath, having been trying to hold it for as long as possible, taking shallow little gasps through my mouth when I could hold it no longer.

I learnt early on that it was always a bad idea to carry a toilet roll with me, because other people in the queue would be asking for pieces and you would end up with none for yourself by the time you got to the front, so I would just bring a few sheets at a time out with me from the cell, and hide them in my pockets. You soon learnt all these lessons. I learnt rule number one within a day of sharing a small cell with Antonio that it was considered unacceptable to take a crap in the cell toilet. It would be less embarrassing to do the necessary while a queue of fellow prisoners waited outside, than to foul your cell-mate's 10-foot by 8-foot personal space.

I had to keep my cigarettes as carefully hidden as my toilet roll. The moment I got out a packet there would be people coming up pestering me for one, so I developed a sly way of sliding them out of the packet out of sight and puffing on them as discreetly as possible. I'd never been a big smoker in the past, never during the day, but in prison it was different. It was the only way to pass the time. Cigarettes were cheap, so giving them away wasn't a problem financially; I just got tired of being constantly pestered. If you gave a guy a cigarette one day, he would be back for another every day after that, and then several times a day. The scroungers would always push their luck to the limit, promising to return the favour 'tomorrow', which never happened. Sometimes I could go downstairs with a pack of twenty and they would all be gone in one hit. The same people would be nagging for money for cups of coffee all the time as well. It was like being surrounded by beggars and unable to escape.

'No money, I have no money,' I kept repeating, although lots of them knew that I did have some.

The continual hassling wore me down, but if I'd given in to every request my weekly allowances would have been gone in an hour.

With 180 people using four showers you could queue for over an hour sometimes to get in one. Obviously, they needed cleaning every day. If that responsibility was given to someone who had upset the other prisoners in some way, they would all go in ahead of him and shit on the floor, smearing it up the walls and everywhere they could reach, just to make his job more unpleasant. The cleaner would then just swill a bucket of water around and most of the mess stayed. Quite often I would prefer to go without a shower, particularly as it was always icy cold water, and would choose to use a bucket in my cell later, in front of whatever cell-mate I had.

The whole prison, which had been like a furnace all summer, became freezing cold as winter drew in, particularly at night, and a cold shower was the last thing you wanted. The water was operated on a button that gave you just a few seconds of spray at a time; so I would jump under it to get wet, then soap myself up, before hitting the button again for a freezing rinse off. I would never want to stand in there in bare feet with the soap scum and other people's hair, semen and shit. I realised that the most important thing to do with one day's phone call was to ask Jane to send me down some rubber flip-flops. The plugholes would often become bunged up and the water levels would rise, shampoo bottles floating on the top, ending up round your ankles. I never felt any cleaner after showering than I had before.

The prison had given me a little pack of throw-away wash things including a sponge, soap, toothbrush, comb, and razor (and condoms, which gave me a bit of a fright, until I realised it was for conjugal visits, not daily use). Everything else had to be bought at the prison shop, which involved more waiting. While you stood in the queue, sometimes for over an hour, people who had no money would be walking up and down, pushing you to buy them something. They would start by asking for fags; if you refused that they would ask for a coffee or a Coke, assuming you would feel you had got off lightly.

These beggars were considered the lowest of the low by other prisoners, but it didn't stop them from trying. Many of them were obviously down-and-outs, toothless, shameless smackheads who would spend the mornings high on their first morphine hits of the day. They would be given two doses a day by the nurse and would spend the time in between walking around like zombies, pestering everyone.

We had to wait for everything: coffee, a shit, the shop, the shower, the phone, the mail, the meals. We waited to be let out of our cells, and then waited to be let back into them, for doors to open and doors to close. We waited for court appearances and visits, but most of all we waited for our freedom. The only time I noticed there was never a queue was when I went to wash my hands at the sink before meals.

Meals were always a scramble of first come, first served: everyone barged through the door, like a herd of cattle being forced through into a milking shed, smelly bodies rubbing up against me, others flicking their long greasy hair in my face. The menu was always the same; with some form of soup every day and hard bread rolls. The soups were made from fish heads and tails or chicken

bones, always watery and never hot, but useful for soften-
ing the bread enough to make it possible to swallow.
There would usually be some sort of dried-up meat dish,
like a shrivelled pork chop or chicken's wings and feet,
very spare ribs or sausages made from yesterday's scraps.
Everything was overcooked. If there was fruit it was
always bruised.

Prisoners, I guess, come at the bottom of the human
food chain, getting whatever is left once paying customers have had theirs through the shops and markets. At
the end of the meal we would scrape whatever was left
into slops bins in the corner of the room, where swarms
of flies would rise up and swirl in the air before settling
down on some new delicacy. At least something came
further down the food chain than us.

Every Wednesday our weekly allowances were put onto
our swipe cards and everyone would queue up at once
for the shop to buy luxuries like phone cards, alcohol-
free beer, bog roll and cigarettes.

I was counting down the days, seeing the magic
number of thirty drawing closer. My friend Peter came
back down to Spain to see how I was doing. I was
impressed that he had gone to so much trouble and was
grateful for the first friendly face I had seen since being
taken out of the passport queue. He spent two full days
travelling just to get a forty-minute visit sitting on the
other side of a glass partition. Another friend, Will, also
made the same trip.

It was hard for Inés to get to see me because she was 300 miles away in Malaga. I was angry that I hadn't been warned I was going to be moved to Madrid. If I had known that, Jane and Catherine could have looked for a local lawyer who would have been able to get in to see me more often. Inés did appear once, combining visiting me with a shopping trip. She bustled in, ladened down with designer bags, assuring me that everything was going to be all right because the paperwork still hadn't arrived from Morocco. 'Just hang in there,' she said, 'we're doing all we can to get you out.'

When you had been in the prison a while you would have regular places where you sat, but in the dining room there were only enough seats for about half the number of people on the wing, so a lot ended up sitting on the floor with their trays of slops.

Getting a chair was always a luxury, even though they were hard plastic, since they were so hard to come by. I got more confident as the days passed and started leaving my jacket on the back of a chair if I went outside to have a cigarette or a walk, in the hope the chair would still be free when I got back. Often it was because the seat I used wasn't popular with other prisoners. It was right by the doors, so there was a constant draft and the noise of the doors continually being opened and closed by remote control from the guardroom, when there were enough people waiting to go in or out. There was also a loud-speaker just above it, constantly crackling into life and shouting out names of prisoners wanted in the office for work, medication, a lawyer's visit or possibly even to be released. It was very seldom they called out the name 'Packwooo!'

As I grew more accustomed to the constant noise, I learnt how to fall asleep with my head slumped over the table in the non-smoking room, to pass a few more hours each day. Usually I would be woken up by my arm going numb underneath me and I would have to wave it around to try to get the blood flowing again.

Thirty days was beginning to feel like three hundred.

Jane

I was so relieved to think that the thirty days were nearly up, knowing that no paperwork had been received
from Morocco and that the chances were improving all
the time that they wouldn't meet their deadline with
Spain in time.

I missed Johnny terribly and it was hard work taking
care of all his affairs, legal and personal, things he needed doing to secure his release, while at the same time
trying to keep up a normal home life for Freya. I was
determined that she wouldn't lose out because of what
was going on and made sure I never missed any school
events and was always there to drop her off and pick her
up as usual. However, there were times when I would be
waiting impatiently for a phone call from John, or would
be tearing my hair out with frustration as I tried to get
through to someone who I thought might be able to
help, when I know I was too near the edge to give her

all the attention she deserved. I waited impatiently for the postman each morning, desperate to see Johnny's handwriting on an envelope, knowing at the same time that his words were quite likely to break my heart all over again when I read them. The life he was describing in prison seemed so far away and he sounded so lonely and worried, but I couldn't stop myself from reading them over and over again, just to feel closer to him. Our phone calls were so hurried and frantic I could often barely remember what we had said once I hung up.

The back room of our terraced house had become like a war room as I collected material that I hoped would help Johnny to prove his innocence if that was necessary, plus information on how to deal with prison in Morocco if everything went wrong. The thought that he might actually end up in a Moroccan prison was terrifying. I felt so helpless; however hard Catherine and I worked at the problem we just didn't seem to be able to get anywhere. We had collected statements from everyone we could think of who knew Johnny or knew anything about the delivery of the *Cygnet*, and had them translated into Spanish and sent down to Inés. She was so confident that the Moroccans would never bother to follow up with the paperwork and our ordeal would soon be over that I couldn't help but feel my morale picking up with every day that passed, despite my underlying fears. I had to be optimistic – otherwise the situation seemed unbearably frightening.

Finally the last day arrived. She was right; the
Moroccans hadn't bothered to send any paperwork
through by the thirty-day deadline. On the eve of the thir-
tieth day, we all prepared ourselves to welcome John home
the following day and I dared to believe that the ordeal
might be nearly over. The Ministry of Justice was due to
close at 8.00 pm and Inés had rung them to check during
the day that nothing had been submitted from Morocco.

'You could fly over and meet him at the prison gate,'
she suggested when she rang to tell me that all was still
going to plan, but I thought it would be better if I waited with Freya for him to get back to the island. Apart
from anything else, we couldn't afford to spend any more
money on the whole mess. Paying Inés had made a serious dent in Johnny's savings and I hadn't been able to do
much work during the previous month to make up for
his lost earnings. It was all proving to be a very expensive mix-up and I knew that Johnny would be very sad
to see that so much of his precious nest egg had already
disappeared. But still, I told myself, as long as the nightmare was nearly over the money didn't matter; we could
always recoup it once Johnny got home, just as long as
he did come home.

Inés rang again at 8.00 pm.

'The Moroccans have placed a phone call to the
Ministry of Justice,' she said. 'They have decided to give
the Moroccan government another forty days to come up
with the paperwork.'

Another forty days? I couldn't believe I'd heard her right. I was stunned, having been led to believe that a simple phone call would not be sufficient for the extradition to go through. In my mind I had imagined welcoming Johnny back home the next day and suddenly he seemed to be a million miles away, sliding beyond reach.

'Why's that?' I asked, my voice quivering close to tears. If I was feeling this sick with disappointment I could hardly imagine how Johnny was going to feel.

'I don't know,' she admitted, obviously surprised by the news herself, and probably embarrassed to have to pass it on after being so confident that our ordeal was nearly over. 'It must be a big case.'

Once she was off the line I looked in the diary to work out when I could hope to see Johnny again. I counted off the days and was horrified to discover that forty days took us to 23 December, two days before Christmas. He had gone away for a late summer holiday and now he wouldn't be back by Christmas? And that was assuming the Spanish didn't decide to extradite him during the next forty days. If that happened, God only knew when I would see him again. I knew how disheartened Johnny had got during the previous thirty days; I wasn't sure how well he was going to stand up to another forty. I knew I couldn't allow myself to despair. I had to stay strong and optimistic for him.

CHAPTER FOUR

John

When Jane told me about the extra forty days I felt for a moment as if someone had punched me in the throat. I was speechless and choking on the end of the phone, unable to take in the full enormity of what I was hearing. I'd only managed to hold onto my sanity during the thirty days because Inés had told me that it was very unlikely the Moroccans would bother to put in the paperwork. I was convinced that once they studied the evidence, or lack of it, they would see the whole case was ridiculous. But if a Spanish judge was willing to give them another forty days, it must mean he thought there was a chance I was guilty, which suggested he hadn't looked at any of the evidence that Inés had put before him.

What if he let another forty days slip past without reading it? If he had been willing to change the thirty-day rule, might he change this new forty-day one as well?

Could he go on putting off the day I would be released indefinitely? Could the old grey-haired inmate be right? Was I going to spend the next year here? When it was such a potentially serious case, where I could be imprisoned for the rest of my life, surely he should at least study the evidence before making these arbitrary decisions?

My head felt like it was splitting open as I tried to work out what this latest development might mean. None of the answers I was coming up with sounded good. I had not been questioned by anyone since talking to the men from Interpol seven years before, I had not even been officially told what the charges were that were being brought against me. What was to stop them holding me like this indefinitely? I felt completely helpless with no one to turn to in order to appeal for justice. I could feel the pressure building up inside me.

Inés did her best and I was taken to court several times on appeals. Each time I sat there, handcuffed and unable to understand a word that was being said, as they shuffled papers around and then took me back to prison to wait another week or two to hear the decision, which was always negative.

At the first appeal there were three judges, but they eventually decided the case was too big for them to deal with – I guess they were more like magistrates, although it was hard to understand the system without understanding the language. It was passed to a higher court of appeal, which Inés said consisted of something like nine judges. I couldn't believe how many people were being involved in something that shouldn't even have been happening. I couldn't believe that any of them could have read any of the evidence that Jane and Inés had been working on: my employment records and references and even my CV with the delivery job on it – hardly the actions of someone knowingly supplying a vessel for drug trafficking. If they had taken the time to read it they would have seen that the whole case was laughable and would have dismissed it immediately. It was so frustrating not being able to communicate with them directly, not to be able to explain to them why it was impossible that I was involved in drug smuggling in any way. It didn't sound to me like Inés was explaining anything to them. She just didn't seem to be standing up to the judges as a British lawyer might do. She had now been paid and it felt like she had grown complacent.

Sometimes I would be told that my case had come up in front of another court and Inés and I wouldn't have even been there, the paperwork being processed in our absence. The great international legal machine was grinding along and there didn't seem to be anything any of us could do to affect its stately progress.

Over the first few months I was at Valdemoro, I was to be moved to nine different cells. I could understand why most of them didn't want to share with me. When you're banged up in a cell with someone for sixteen or more hours at a time, the least you want is someone who can speak the same language. I knew no Spanish, and never expected to stay there long enough for it to be worthwhile learning, so no one wanted to share with me and I was left in a sort of limbo. It was safer for me to just play dumb. My life had taken on an unbearable monotony. A motorway ran past, close to the windows of the cells, the vehicle roar constantly echoing off the walls. I could just see the outside world from the window, over the 30-foot concrete walls, topped off with coils of razor-bladed wire, but my own world had shrunk to a succession of sweat boxes, cells and exercise yards full of shit. I could have been anywhere in the world by that time, a hundred miles from home or a thousand. Aeroplanes on the flight path into Madrid airport would come in low, making the building shake, and the train tracks added their own contribution to the general noise level, which was endless.

Prisoners wanting to communicate with one another on different wings would write notes, wrap them round old used batteries, secure them with tiny pieces of precious sticky tape and lob them over the walls into the next courtyard. Anyone finding one of these messages would quickly pass it on to whoever it was addressed to. Most of it was inside information about drugs, who had them and where they were stashed.

I was with the German for three weeks before he was moved out, and I then spent a whole day running around the 180 inmates on the wing, trying to find a suitable replacement before new arrivals came and I had no choice but to go in with whatever nutcase they allocated me to. That was when I met Chris, a Nigerian, who I was to spend the best part of the following eight months with. He was a commodity broker, buying and selling goods like rubber and cloth in bulk and he was in prison for some sort of fraud, although he claimed he was innocent. Most inmates claimed that, but with Chris I believed it. He was on remand, waiting for his handwriting to be analysed in order to prove his case.

'Eight months I've been waiting for the results,' he told me. He said he was willing to pay himself to have it done privately. 'We could have the result in a day, but they won't allow it. Anyone can do it in ten minutes with a computer, but I have to wait for the authorities to get their act together.'

They came to him at one stage and told him they would free him if he admitted his guilt.

'I'm not admitting any guilt,' he said, appalled at the prospect. 'If I'm found guilty of fraud they'll take away my trading licence and I'll be finished. I'm innocent and I will keep going till I've proved it.'

We certainly weren't a match made in heaven, but both of us knew we were better off with each other than with virtually anyone else on the wing. At least we could communicate in the same language, even if we got on each other's nerves a lot of the time. He was a big chap and lived on the top bunk and his feet were always dangling over the side, blocking my view of the tiny TV in the corner. Little things like that can start to niggle when you're locked up with someone for hours at a time. The advantage of being on the top bunk was that you had a bit more privacy, although the downside was that you had the bother of having to climb up and down the whole time. Chris liked an argument and would contradict virtually everything I said, even the most trivial comment, which became tiring. His favourite saying, whenever I complained about anything, was: 'Well, that's your problem. Get used to it. This is prison.'

We paid 12 euros a week for the rental of our television from another inmate. He and I were always arguing about what we were going to watch since he was happy to stare at the football all the time and sometimes I wanted to watch something different, even if it was just adverts. Most weeks there would be disputes over payment when we would find out we had both paid the television owner with cigarettes and he would claim we hadn't given him enough. I kept notes but he was always arguing with us and in the end we would become confused ourselves about what we had actually paid or what we still owed him.

Chris gave up smoking while he was in Valdemoro, which showed considerable strength of character, but it meant it wasn't really fair for me to smoke in the cell in front of him. I had trouble sleeping, waking up every couple of hours, and I liked to smoke half a cigarette at moments like that, before trying to get back to sleep. He slept so soundly he never woke up, so I would stand at the window to get rid of the smell, staring at the night sky as I puffed surreptitiously away. He slept so soundly I used to be able to do all my washing after he had nodded off without disturbing him.

After lunch every day we would be banged up in our cells again. I would try to get there first to give the floor a quick sweep, and maybe even a slosh around with the mop and bucket so that it would be dry before my cellmate, Chris, returned. He never could see the point of all that cleaning and he would walk about all over it. He did have a point. Sometimes I even cleaned the window, so we had something to look at, but with everyone above throwing out things like fish oil from tuna tins it soon became opaque with dirt again.

'What's the point of cleaning things in prison,' Chris said, 'when they're just going to get dirty again?'

He carried his theory through to his bedding, which he never bothered to send to the laundry. Every couple of weeks we could put items like bedding, jeans and shirts into the laundry system, but his theory was that he would rather do it himself, since it all got lumped in together with everyone else's. I had to admit I never did like the idea of my bedding being washed with other people's. It never did come back smelling particularly fresh, but at least it was clean. Chris never got round to washing his, mainly because we were forbidden washing lines. His pillow and sheets were stained brown and smelt. Lying in the bunk below him I would be showered with clouds of dust particles of dead skin, food crumbs and pubic hair every time he rolled over. I would be able to watch them glistening in the beam of my little adjustable lamp as they fell.

After lunch I would wash out my socks and pants, so they could dry on the washing line I had constructed from half a dozen boot laces. They would be dry for me to put them back on by the time the screws came to open the doors again a couple of hours later. I didn't want trouble with an illegal line but I couldn't think of any other way to get things dry.

All afternoon I would doze to the constant sounds of Spanish television, voices shouting to one another between windows and Chris's snores from the top bunk, trying to imagine what my life had been like before. I would mentally drive my car around the winding island roads or walk Badger on a sunny afternoon.

To pass the time one afternoon I drew pencil lines on the cell floor, following the shadows thrown by the bars at the window, and timed how long it took for the sun to pass over. A week later I had drawn a full sundial.

Chris never seemed to have any trouble getting to sleep. He would usually be snoring again by nine at night, and I would be tossing and turning for another three hours before my brain would finally allow me to drift off.

I had learned that there was a code of conduct among prisoners that you didn't blatantly steal other people's personal stuff. One day when I came back my jacket had gone from the back of the chair. I knew it wouldn't be acceptable to go complaining to the officers, but I needed to get the jacket back because it was my pillow and, more importantly, it had my irreplaceable list of phone numbers. I had also left my phone card and the card I used to buy things from the shop in the pocket, along with some tapes Jane had sent me, which I was keeping for when I managed to get a Walkman. I told my cellmate, Chris, and a few other people and they hunted around the wing but had no luck.

The next day the bloke who worked in the shop told another British guy that someone had been in trying to use all the credit left on my card. It was quite normal for people to do that, giving their card to someone else to avoid having to queue themselves, but something about him alerted the man's suspicions. It would have taken him years to get that job, he would not want to risk losing it, plus he would have had his own scam going, which he wouldn't have wanted uncovered. The guy he pointed out was a Spanish smackhead who was new on the wing. He had no teeth and his brain was obviously messed up on drugs. Word got around that he was the culprit and he started to get a bit of flak from other people. Occasionally there were thefts from the cells and the stolen goods would be moved off to other wings by people working in the kitchens and sold, but this guy seemed to have kept my stuff for himself.

Realising he was under suspicion and panicking, he dumped my phone card and a few other clues from my pockets in the toilets. That afternoon, during bang-up, Chris told an officer what was going on, even though I didn't want to involve the staff and turn it into a big thing, risking being seen as a grass. No one liked a cell thief, but a grass was worse.

The officer went to see the lad, who denied it all, saying he found my shop card on the floor. Chris and I were then taken to his cell to see if I could find my jacket or identify anything else that was mine. The moment I walked through the door I saw the three tapes that had been in my pocket lying on his bunk. Two of them were music tapes that Jane had got from my car, but the third was a recording of television programmes about me that Jane had sent down, with my name written on it. I showed the guard, who then took the junkie down to the office and started interrogating him. It wasn't long before the pressure got to him and he crumbled and admitted my jacket was hidden in his cell under a load of rubbish.

The theft was a rare occurrence, even though the prison was full of thieves. There were always harsh retributions dished out by the inmates and I had witnessed several beatings, but the incident still made me feel vulnerable because it reminded me that no matter how little I had in the world, there were still going to be people who would want to take it away from me.

Not being able to speak the language caused all sorts of difficulties in my daily life as well as the legal issues. When I developed a nasty rash from all the filth around the prison, I asked to see the prison nurse. I took Chris, my cell-mate, with me to interpret, but she shooed him out of the room, saying she would manage in English. She then spoke to me in Spanish and refused to compromise. When I told her I didn't understand she became angry and told me that if I couldn't be bothered to learn Spanish she couldn't be bothered to treat me.

If I had known from the beginning how long I was going to be in Valdemoro I might have made more of an effort to learn the language, but I was always expecting to go home at any moment so it never seemed worth it, and then it almost became a point of principle. In truth I was just too depressed to be able to think of anything like that.

The rash eventually went away of its own accord, but months later when I felt a lump in my groin I really panicked, convinced I had got cancer and would end up dying in some terrible prison hospital. I tried again to talk to the nurse, but she was still adamant that unless I could explain my problem in Spanish she wasn't interested.

I told Jane during my next rushed phone call home and she rang the embassy for advice.

'If you have money,' they told her, 'you should probably pay for an outside doctor to come in.'

By that stage I was losing the will to live and I thought that if I was going to die of cancer there wasn't much I could do about it. It was a stupid attitude, but I was beginning to lose all logic and reason. I certainly didn't think I could afford to be hiring private doctors on top of everything else. What capital I now had left was going to be needed just to see me through till I got home.

The lump also subsided of its own accord, taking my immediate fears with it. But at the back of my mind I couldn't help wondering what would happen if I was extradited to Morocco and then something more serious went wrong with my health. The thought of being ill so far from home was deeply frightening, especially when I had all day and night to think about it.

Jane

I was now feeling as panic stricken as Johnny. In the darkest moments of the night, while he was lying awake on his prison bed, listening to his cell-mate's snores, I was lying alone in bed at home with my mind churning over and over everything that was happening. I realised we were in real danger of not being able to stop the extradition from happening and I was terrified that if that went ahead I might not see him again for years. Just when life had seemed to be getting so good, this bolt had arrived out of the blue and shattered all our plans and dreams. If Inés, who was supposed to be an expert on the subject, was shocked by their decision to extend the deadline by forty days, then anything might happen. Her reassurances that everything would be all right no longer seemed so reassuring.

As the only person he could communicate with most days, I felt a terrible weight of responsibility for Johnny's fate. As far as Inés was concerned he was just another client. I was sure she wanted to help, but if it all went wrong she would still be going back to her own home every evening, and would still have her job the next day. We, on the other hand, could have our whole lives destroyed.

If anyone was going to force through his case it was going to have to be Catherine and me. We shared all the responsibilities, even though Catherine had her own job and family to run at the same time as helping us. Sometimes it all just seemed too much to cope with. We had both spent hundreds of hours working on trying to find a solution.

Whenever I spoke to him, Johnny always had so many questions he wanted Inés to answer, such as who had she spoken to, what had they said, had she put this point to them or that one? And I would have to try to get the answers from her before I next spoke to him. With my lack of Spanish and Inés' broken English our communications were always a struggle. Whenever I managed to get through to her on the phone she always seemed to be in a rush to get somewhere else to another client or another meeting. I felt I was being a nuisance continually trying to get information that she probably didn't even have, but I needed an ally. I needed to believe she knew what she was doing and that Johnny's fate was in safe hands.

She kept using phrases like, 'But it's a delicate matter.' I would know, once I had hung up after talking to her, that nothing I had learned would be of any comfort to Johnny. She would write to him every so often from her office in Malaga, updating him on what was happening and encouraging him, but it was always information I had passed on to him weeks before and the encouragement was beginning to seem like a triumph of optimism over experience. We didn't feel confident that she had the same feeling of urgency that we did. The stress was building all the time.

Catherine and I talked on the phone for hours on end, and did our best to shield Frances from as many of the complications and disappointments as possible. I was now realising it was too much for Catherine and me to handle on our own in England; we were out of our depth and needed some serious advice from someone who understood the whole extradition situation.

In the course of my researches I had come across a charity called Fair Trials Abroad, which was launched by a lawyer called Stephen Jakobi OBE in 1994, specifically to help people like Johnny obtain fair trials. When I rang I got straight through to Stephen himself. He listened very carefully to everything I had to say and seemed to understand all my worries perfectly. His son was actually making a boat delivery that day so he could understand the ramifications that a case like this could have on the whole yachting and boating industry. If anyone who ever delivered a boat to another country could be held responsible for whatever the owners chose to do with the boat later, the whole industry could grind to a halt. He was a sailor himself and completely understood everything I was telling him. He assured me he would be happy to help in any way he could. Because his company was a charity, I didn't have to worry unduly about money for the first time since Johnny disappeared, and this only added to my relief at finding him. The fact that the director himself was going to take our case on personally was also really encouraging. Only a week or two later did we discover that he had 360 such cases of presumed innocents abroad on his books. Our hopes were constantly being lifted like this, only to be followed by disappointment.

'It would probably be wise not to rattle any cages in Morocco unnecessarily at this stage,' Stephen suggested. 'Just in case it proves to be a storm in a teacup. They haven't been able to come up with anything in thirty days, another forty probably won't produce anything either. We should probably just let sleeping dogs lie at the moment. Let's see what happens on the fortieth day and not risk goading the Moroccan authorities into action. There is still a chance they might not even bother to fill out the paperwork and the Spanish will just send him home.'

The priority now was to make Johnny as comfortable as possible at Valdemoro while he endured another forty days. One of his biggest problems as the winter approached was the cold, since he still only had the clothes he had taken with him for the windsurfing holiday. Rather than just send off an anonymous parcel, I decided I would make a trip down to see him. I had felt terribly torn between wanting to be with him in his hour of need, and wanting to stay at home, keeping the campaign running at full speed. I decided the time had come to take the plunge and go.

The information I was sent by the British Embassy in Madrid warned that visitors might be strip-searched on the way in. The thought of the rubber gloves going on really worried me. I confided my fears to the woman at the embassy.

'Don't worry,' she said. 'It hardly ever happens. The only woman I know who had that happen had managed to smuggle a mobile phone in on a previous visit somehow.'

Just the thought of smuggling a mobile phone in a private orifice almost brought tears to my eyes. Imagine if it had gone off!

There was also the question of the money. We had already spent £8,000 on the lawyer and I wasn't getting much work done while I was concentrating my days on trying to build up evidence for Johnny. A trip to Spain for me was going to be another drain on his dwindling resources, and who knew how much more money we would need before the whole ordeal was over.

If there were still any doubts lingering in my mind, the next phone call washed them away. John was sounding worse with every conversation – desperately worried about staying warm, about staying healthy and about staying sane. We both felt so helpless and distressed when we heard one another's voices. Every call was so intense and so short there was never any time to really talk properly or let our emotions loose. I wanted to do something positive, and I wanted to see him again. Hearing his voice in our short, frantic phone calls was like a torture, like a reminder of who he was without him actually being there. I felt that if I didn't see him and touch him I might go mad with worry and loneliness.

My brother, Miles, who works as a painter and decorator, agreed to take a few days off to come with me, which was a huge relief. Travelling is a stressful enough activity at the best of times, but to be going into a place as alien as a foreign prison on my own would have been doubly daunting.

Organising the necessary permission to visit was the next nightmare. First I had to arrange a time with Johnny. He would then have to put the request in to the prison authorities. If they agreed he would tell me and I would have to contact the embassy in Madrid, who would then send me a letter of introduction in Spanish through the post, which I had to take with me. I was warned that the letter had to be worded in a particular way or the authorities might refuse to accept it when I got there. I then had to plan an itinerary that would get us to the prison as quickly and cheaply as possible, so that I would be away from Freya for the least possible amount of time. At least when I was busy organising the trip I had less time to think about Johnny sitting in the prison, not knowing what was going on or what was going to happen to him; at least I was able to fill most of my days and thoughts with activity and distract myself from the ache that seemed permanently lodged in my heart.

The thought of flying into the country that Johnny had innocently set off for a couple of months before was frightening. While I had no reason to assume something bad would happen to us when the authorities discovered we were there, I no longer felt confident about anything. After what had happened to Johnny, I realised that you can never be sure of what's going to happen next. I was desperate to see him, to try to comfort him in any way I could, but I was also nervous of how I would find him. How would be look after so many weeks of misery, worry and suffering from the prison conditions?

John

The cold was only one of my problems, but it was becoming increasingly difficult to bear as winter took a firm grip on the exposed walls of the prison. There was now snow falling across the plains and the terrible heat I had found so difficult to cope with at the beginning of my imprisonment had started to become a fond memory.

When Jane told me she was planning to come down and see me I could feel my spirits lifting. It would be the first time I'd seen her face since I'd been moved to Valdemoro, but she would also be a reminder of just how much I stood to lose if everything went wrong for me at the end of forty days. To have waited so long to find the love of my life, and then to know there was a strong possibility we would be parted again for years, was almost too painful to think about.

I knew what a big effort it was for her to get away and travel to a prison in the middle of nowhere, and I was deeply grateful. In my optimistic moments I thought the visit would be no more than a bit of a laugh. Having got this far through the ordeal I only had about another two weeks to hold out before the forty days were up and I would be able to go home for Christmas. I also really needed the jumpers and other supplies she was going to be bringing with her, like some smarter clothes for me to wear on court appearances. I wasn't sure the trip was a wise use of our precious remaining money, but I no longer cared; I just wanted to see her.

Because it was a 'conjugal rights' visit, we would be allowed to spend some hours together in a room with a bed, which was another added bonus, but also made the impending visit heavy with the weight of both our expectations. So many things might go wrong and spoil these few precious hours.

As the day got closer I found myself becoming increasingly nervous. I told myself it was ridiculous; why should I feel nervous about seeing my girlfriend? But I had butterflies in my stomach, like a teenager going out on a first date. We had both been through so much since we last met, would we still be able to connect in the easy way we had when we were relaxed and on our home territory? And how would Jane react to the way I was looking – and smelling?

I had nothing to distract me from thinking about the visit every waking hour, imagining everything we would say to each other, what she would look like, how it would feel to hold Jane in my arms again after so many weeks. We wouldn't have to talk about the legal side of things because that was all nearly over; at least, I hoped it was.

My biggest worry was that she might get turned away at the checkpoint for not having exactly the right paperwork. I knew how vindictive and petty the guards could be sometimes. Other prisoners had told me how they often sent visiting women away for the smallest mistakes, even when they had travelled all the way across Spain, sometimes bringing all their children with them. As the day drew closer I hardly dared to believe it was actually going to happen.

John's family: (from left to right) Catherine, Frances, John Senior and John, 1976

Jane's family: (back row, from left to right) Miles and Leona; (front row, from left to right) Jane and Laura, 1970

John, Badger and Jane

John on the marina, Cowes Week,
August 2002

John and Peter racing their 7-metre
catamaran, Cowes Week

The HMS *Cygnet*, soon after her launch in the 1970s

Valdemoro maximum security prison, Madrid, as seen from the outside, July 2005

John awaiting his first appeal hearing in the Spanish Courts in Madrid, 31 March 2005

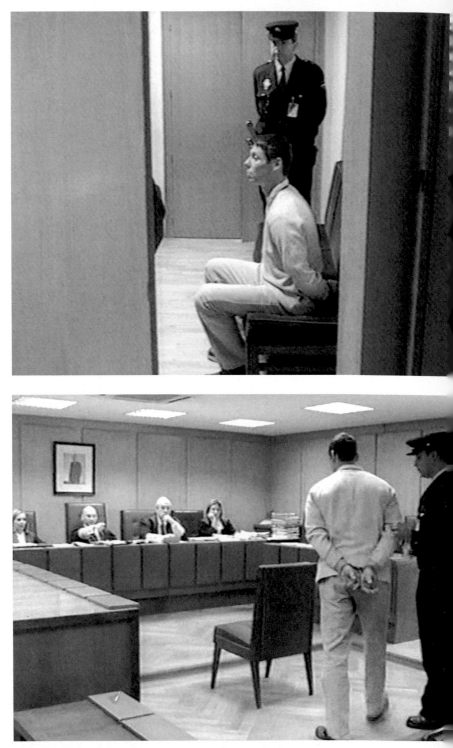

John being taken into the Spanish courtroom to appear before judges, 31 March 2005

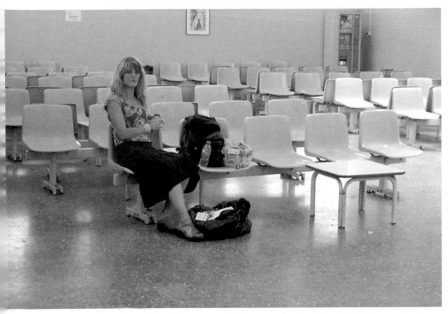

Jane in the visitor's waiting room at Valdemoro for her fourth visit, September 2005

Kenitra civil prison, Morocco,
October 2005

Salé prison, Morocco,
October 2005

Jane and Catherine at a news conference in London, 11 November 2004 (*Photo: Stefan Rousseau/PA/Empics*)

John's lawyer, Jason McCue, 2006

Handing in letters to the Spanish embassy in London, before heading to the Moroccan embassy: (back row, from left to right) Margaret Quigley, Terry Fisher, Jane's sister Laura and Ollie Bennet; (middle row, from left to right) Jane's mother Leona, Catherine and her husband Andrew; (front row, from left to right) Stephen Jakobi OBE from Fair Trials Abroad, Frances and Jane, February 2005

John hugs Jane as they
are reunited at Heathrow
airport, 18 November 2005
(*Photo: Johnny Green/PA*)

Reunited at Heathrow airport: (from left to right) Frances, John, Jane and Catherine,
18 November 2005 (*Photo: Johnny Green/PA*)

John and Jane, London, October 2006
(*Photo: ok?design*)

Jane

The practical details of the trip filled my days, but in the quiet of the night, as I lay awake thinking about Johnny, I felt a knot of excitement at the prospect of actually seeing his face again. On the morning that I was due to leave I woke early, feeling tense with excitement and worried that I would get all the way there, only to be turned away at the gates on some technicality.

Miles and I agreed to meet at Gatwick airport, and I took the ferry across to Southampton to catch the train up. I was laden down with things Johnny had asked for, like books, magazines and clothes. As I waited on Southampton station platform, surrounded by bags, my phone rang. It was Catherine.

'I just heard from Inés,' she said. I knew from the tone of her voice this wasn't going to be good news. 'The paperwork has been submitted from Morocco.'

I felt sick. 'What does that mean exactly?'

'Apparently they've crossed all the "t"s and dotted all the "i"s,' she said. 'It looks like John won't be home for Christmas.'

'Does he know yet?'

'No. You'll have to tell him when you get there.'

The visit I had been so looking forward to suddenly took on the shape of an ordeal as I realised this might be the last time I would be able to see him for years. Surrounded by commuters, I headed for London, trying to hold back the tears. In the few hours we were going to be allowed to spend alone together I was going to have to tell him that all his hopes of an imminent release had just evaporated, and that he would now almost certainly be sent to Morocco to stand trial for a crime that they were convinced he had committed. It didn't seem possible that things could have gotten so out of control. It was like some nonsensical story from *Alice in Wonderland*, where nothing anyone said quite added up. All logic had disappeared from our lives and we were left with a bunch of international officials and experts mouthing platitudes that made no sense but who still had the power to ruin our lives. The more we tried to point out the illogicality of it all, the less they seemed to hear our words and arguments.

Miles was great. Not only did he provide me with the moral support I needed, he carried my bags and treated the whole trip as a job. At the most stressful moments, when the whole experience threatened to overwhelm me, he became my brain, steering me through whatever had to be done as I plodded on in a trance, trying to imagine how Johnny was going to take the news.

Valdemoro (Valley of the Moors) is about 20 miles outside Madrid. I had planned the trip over the internet, equipping myself with city maps and train timetables. As I got ready I had to pack a case of stuff for John, as well as my own travelling case, and another for Freya so she could go and stay with my mum and sister. Because of flight times, and ferries back to the island, it was going to be a two- or three-day trip, and it would involve getting across Madrid on the underground system and changing trains with no Spanish, no idea where we were, and a load of luggage to carry with us.

I had booked a hotel in a quaint little town called Pinto, which Peter had worked out was the closest town to the prison. The hotel was nice and there was a square of cafés where people congregated in the evenings, but any charm it might have held was lost on me as I prepared myself for the ordeal of having to crush Johnny's hopes yet again.

It was a taxi ride from the hotel out to the prison, a daunting, ugly fortress standing in the middle of the plains. Miles accompanied me all the way to the waiting room, but I had to leave him there and go on through the many doors on my own, surrendering my passport and handing over my paperwork before they would let me into the actual prison building and into a waiting room filled with women and children, many of them crying or jabbering angrily in Spanish. My body was shaking uncontrollably with nerves. All I wanted to do was turn around and run all the way home, but it was too late for that now. I just had to focus my thoughts on seeing Johnny.

The floor was littered with cigarette ends, despite the 'no smoking' signs on every wall. I had been told to be at the prison two hours before my designated visiting time, but there were no staff there to deal with me, so I just had to sit and wait. As the minutes dragged by, I was so desperate for a cigarette to calm my nerves I decided it was worth the risk of ignoring the instructions and lit up. No one gave me a second glance and I inhaled gratefully.

Just before I went through into the main prison I put in one last call to Catherine. We had been in this together from the beginning and I almost felt that she was there with me as I walked through the gates to the place we both felt we knew so much about, even though we had never been there. What made it worse was I knew I had two 50-euro notes taped inside my boots. It was hard to believe that someone who never even walked on the cracks in the pavement was smuggling currency into a maximum-security prison, but that was what I had been reduced to because I knew Johnny needed the money desperately to pay for his protection against violent maniacs. The thought of being caught made me almost faint with fear.

I had to walk through metal detectors, which, thank God, didn't go off. On a later visit they would go off and I would be forced to strip right down, even taking off my bra because of the wiring. This time I got through okay, but I was still shivering with anxiety.

The prison guards, when they finally turned their attention to herding us through, seemed to want to do as little as they possibly could They also seemed to make the rules up as they went along. Johnny had warned me to expect that. They were particularly impatient with anyone who didn't speak Spanish. They acted most of the time as if we were invisible, smoking and chatting to one another just feet away from where we stood, silently and patiently waiting for them to take pity on us and open another door or lift yet another barrier. A little power seemed to have left them intoxicated.

Every so often we would find ourselves walking through what seemed like patches of barren scrubland right at the core of the prison, awash with litter. The guards directed us on what seemed like an endless journey through door after door before we got to our destination, yet as soon as the visits were over we found ourselves back outside the walls after just a few steps. It was like some sort of strange optical illusion, as if they were deliberately trying to intimidate and disorientate us by taking us the longest route possible. Johnny had no idea how close the outside world actually was, being lost as he was inside a hidden one.

Usually prisoners were allowed two conjugal visits a month, lasting an hour and a half each. Because I was flying all the way in from England the embassy had arranged for us to have three hours in one go. Every moment that they delayed me in getting to him was agony. I was terrified they would end up wasting the whole three hours on their endless procedures and security checks. Finally we reached the rooms set aside for conjugal visits.

John

My heart was thumping as I was taken to the room to
meet Jane. I used to get nervous just waiting to hear her
voice over the phone, never mind a face-to-face meeting
after so long. My palms were sweating as I wondered if
anything would have gone wrong on the way to make
them cancel the visit. And had she heard anything new
that she would be able to relay to me? If so, would I be
hearing good news or bad? The tensions had been building inside my head for the whole twenty-four hours
since our last telephone call. There was so much waiting
and it always seemed to be terminated with bad news,
another setback, another disappointment. What sort of a
mixture of emotions would this visit bring?

I was determined that we wouldn't spend the whole
three hours talking about the business of getting me out,
that we would use the time to re-establish our relationship, to enjoy seeing one another. I wanted to have a visit

that I could think about for however many more days I was trapped inside Valdemoro. Having good things to think about was crucial when you were trying to cling on to your sanity.

I felt overwhelmed as I walked in and saw her. She was just as beautiful as I remembered. But her expression wasn't the one I had expected to see. She looked drained and exhausted and could barely raise a smile.

'Bad news, Johnny,' she said almost immediately, obviously desperate to get it out of the way as soon as possible. 'Some sort of paperwork has come through from Morocco. Inés says they've decided to go ahead with the extradition.'

My spirits plummeted. I couldn't believe they would actually send an innocent European out to Morocco to face some trumped-up charges. Surely the Spanish would find a reason to overrule the Moroccans? Whatever happened next, it meant my ordeal would almost certainly not be over at the end of the latest forty-day deadline. It seemed they could keep on inventing reasons to put off releasing me. I still hadn't been charged with anything, or even questioned by anyone in authority, but decisions were being made about my fate by people I had never even met, and who apparently knew nothing about my situation.

'What does Stephen Jakobi think?' I asked.

'He doesn't think Spain will actually extradite you,' Jane reassured me. 'He says we need to play it for as long as possible over here; keep on appealing until the judge actually looks at the evidence we've been submitting.'

I was pleased to think that someone with Stephen Jakobi's experience didn't think I would ever actually be extradited, but the thought of being stuck in Valdemoro while they all argued about it was almost as bad. If it had taken us two months to get to this situation, which was basically no further on than the day I was arrested, how many more months would it be before the various authorities found a solution that would save everyone's face? It could be at least another two months, if not longer. I had met so many inmates who had been waiting for up to a year for their cases to be decided.

The only good thing about receiving this latest news was that at least Jane was actually there to share it with me, and to provide comfort and sympathy — things I hadn't realised I had been missing so badly until she put her arms around me for a hug. Being intimate felt strange and awkward after so long apart, almost like we were on a first date with nothing to laugh about in order to break the ice.

Jane

We both cried as Johnny walked into the visiting room, partly from relief at me having finally got there, after expecting to be stopped or turned back at each stop through the system. I was shaking from the stress of the trip and the news I knew I was going to have to break. The strain of the previous weeks had been so intense for both of us and suddenly the dams that we had built to contain our emotions burst open.

He looked like he hadn't slept for weeks. Lines of anxiety were etched in his face. He seemed constantly nervous, on edge and incapable of relaxing. It was like he had forgotten how it felt to be in a safe environment with someone who loved him unconditionally. He seemed to find it hard to believe that I was happy to dedicate every spare moment I had to getting him free.

Once I'd told him the bad news and he had recovered from the initial shock, we talked for a while, and then made love. We were both eager for the human contact and warmth as much as the sex, but it wasn't a very happy experience for either of us – we stared into each other's eyes, knowing it could be for the last time. It was also hard to enjoy making love with the clanging of doors going on all around, and with the knowledge that there were two guards standing right outside the door, just feet away from where we were lying, holding what sounded like a normal conversation.

There was another couple having a furious row somewhere nearby, which we could hear clearly through the unglazed window. The row of rooms for conjugal visits was opposite another row of rooms designated for families with children to meet in. We weren't individuals to the authorities, just statistics from among the paperwork of the prison system.

Lying together on the bed wasn't really about the sex, more about holding each other, being close to someone you trust and love and enjoying an intimacy both of us had been missing ever since Johnny first went away. I wanted to comfort him, rather like I might have wanted to comfort Freya when she was little and had found the world to be less kind than she had previously believed it to be, but knew that ultimately I was helpless in the face of the forces that we were facing up to. Talking to me was Johnny's only chance of letting his emotions loose; he certainly couldn't allow them to show once he was back on the wing among the other inmates.

To me the little visiting room seemed cold, sordid and dirty, but for Johnny it was luxury compared with the cells he was used to. It was the first time he'd looked in a proper mirror for months. The only ones in the prison were sheets of stainless steel, which only gave a hazy, distorted reflection. Presumably the authorities didn't want to risk putting glass on the wings, when it could so easily be smashed and turned into lethal weapons. Not that the sight of his worried, strained face was too encouraging. There was a hard, wooden double bed, covered with sheets stamped with the words 'Valdemoro', and a disgusting old bathroom suite. The authorities had even provided condoms in the room, which was thoughtful and a bit surprising in a Catholic country.

Johnny had brought in a little picnic of the sorts of foods he was allowed to buy in the prison shop, like a small pack of low alcohol beer, biscuits, sweets, olives and crisps. He had perfected a way of making a cocktail from a packet of crisps mixed with a tin of olives and stuffed anchovies, the olive oil soaking into the crisps. Although he was allowed to take things into the room, he wasn't allowed to take anything out, in case I was trying to smuggle something in to him. In fact I was smuggling him some money, which he quickly secreted about his person.

He asked me to take a pile of papers with me when I left, including all the letters I had written him over the previous months. He wanted to have as little stuff in the cell as possible, fearful that things would go missing if he had too much to carry next time he had to move cells. I was touched that he didn't want to lose my love letters. Seeing how much they meant to him made me glad I had spent the time sending so many. I went away at the end of the visit with almost as much stuff as I'd arrived with.

We soon returned to talking about how we were going to get him freed before they took him to Morocco. It was all either of us ever thought about any more – always lurking just below the surface, even when we were talking about other things. Johnny had made a list of priority jobs that he needed me to do, being worried that if he relied on his memory at such an intense moment he might forget something crucial.

The news about the extradition was like a lead weight on our spirits, which grew heavier as the minutes ticked away. Would this be the last time we ever saw each other? Would Johnny ever see his mother again before he finally managed to get his freedom? Frances was becoming increasingly frail, not helped by all the worry about her son's future.

The three hours went past so quickly. A guard banged on the door and we looked at each other, guessing our time was up. In fact there were ten minutes of visiting time left, so we could prepare ourselves to step back outside. Those ten minutes were an agony. The harder we willed the minutes to pass slowly, the quicker they seemed to slip through our fingers. Then the door opened and I was instructed to step out.

Walking away and leaving Johnny there ripped my heart out. I couldn't look back at him once I'd started to walk away because of the sight of him left alone in that place would have made me sob, and I was determined not to do that. There was so much misery all around, with everyone wailing and crying as they were parted from their loved one, and I didn't want to sink into that. I wanted them to see that they couldn't break us – not that they cared, or even noticed. The prisoners were all standing at the doors of the visiting rooms as their wives and families reluctantly left them. To get down the corridor I had to brush past them and I wondered what crimes they were inside for. Were they murderers? I felt unsettled and fearful of the unknown world. I could understand all the more clearly why Johnny so often sounded frightened and disorientated on the phone. After the visit I would be better able to picture his situation and understand his fears.

The prisoners had to wait while the visitors were all moved out of the area, then they would be escorted back to the wing, after being strip-searched to check we hadn't managed to smuggle anything in. I hoped Johnny had hidden the money well. I half walked and half ran back to Miles, who had been sitting patiently in the waiting area. I was trying to move as fast as I could without drawing too much attention to myself or looking guilty or suspicious. All I wanted was to get away from Valdemoro as quickly as possible.

'Let's get out of here, fast,' I said the moment I saw him. 'We need to call a taxi,' Miles said.

He'd been waiting hours since I had first disappeared into the system, with no idea exactly when I would reappear. He was as anxious to get out as I was, glad to be away from people constantly hassling him for money and cigarettes. The guards reluctantly agreed to help by making the call for us and then we were sent outside to wait in the cold. We stood outside the gates, in the middle of nowhere, just praying that the cab would show up as requested. Waiting for a taxi is always tedious, a thousand times more so when you have no idea what you will do if it fails to show up. After what seemed like an age it arrived and we climbed gratefully in, neither of us looking back at the prison as the driver sped away.

About half an hour after leaving the prison my feelings of fear, anxiety and sadness hardened into anger. Why should we be being put through all this agony when Johnny had done nothing wrong? Why should I be forced to leave my daughter and come all this way, just to be treated like a criminal myself? Why should we be forced to spend our life's savings on trying to prove something that was blatantly obvious to anyone who took the trouble to examine the facts? It all seemed so unjust, yet no one in authority was doing anything to help. Anger is a good emotion for keeping you going, forcing you to fight on, steeling you not to even think of giving up.

*

Once back on the Isle of Wight I was determined to increase my efforts to get Johnny out of Valdemoro. Having actually seen the place, I could understand how crucial it was to get him returned to normal life. Now that it was obvious he was not going to get out at the end of the forty days, Stephen Jakobi said there was no longer anything to be gained from keeping quiet and avoiding rocking the political boat. Now, he said, was the time for us to make active use of all the material we had been preparing while we waited to see what would happen. We had hoped we would never need to use it, but that was obviously not going to be the case. We were going to have to start making as loud a noise as possible, attracting as much media attention as possible, embarrassing whoever needed to be embarrassed. This was our last chance to shout for help to anyone who was willing and able to give it.

Stephen arranged to go to Morocco himself, with us just paying his expenses, in order to set up meetings with the British Ambassador in Rabat, the Premier Council to Europe, and even the Moroccan Minister of Justice and Director of Criminal Affairs and Pardons, trying to make the situation clearer to them from our perspective. He wanted to get to the bottom of exactly why they were so determined to put Johnny on trial when all the evidence pointed to him knowing nothing about the boat after he left it in Agadir and even less about the people who had bought it. Catherine's husband, Andrew, went with him to provide moral support and to represent the family. They found a local English-speaking lawyer, called Ben, and put him on standby in case the worst happened and Spain actually allowed Johnny to be taken there.

When they returned, they reported that everyone had been very hospitable and polite to them, and seemed encouraged.

'They kept assuring me there was nothing to worry about,' Stephen said. 'Everyone I met promised John will be treated fairly when he gets there, and given a fair trial.'

It was nice to know they intended to treat him well, but it still didn't answer the question of why they wanted him there at all, when we could prove he and his fellow crew members came straight back to England after leaving Agadir and had no record of ever having anything to do with drugs or the Cali Cartel, that they were regular working guys. The fact that we were beginning to talk about 'when' Johnny got to Morocco rather than 'if', was chilling.

Ben, the Moroccan lawyer, had carried on talking to the prosecutor after Stephen and Andrew returned to England and he sent news that the prosecutor was willing to do a deal. It seemed they had found a way to save some face.

'They say they're willing to drop the extradition warrant,' he said, 'if John agrees to go to Morocco as a free man and answer questions.'

The next time I was talking to Johnny I told him what they were asking.

'Okay,' he said, 'I'll do that. Why not? I've got nothing to hide. It would be better than spending another year sat here, trying to fight it, and then being sent anyway.'

I relayed his reaction back to Stephen and Ben and they started making the arrangements. Things were moving along, until the Foreign Office heard what was happening and the British Embassy in Morocco rang the judge direct to tell him they wanted some sort of guarantee that they wouldn't just arrest Johnny the moment he arrived in their country and throw him in jail. The embassy were worried they wouldn't be able to protect Johnny's rights if he went to Morocco under his own steam. The judge informed them he wasn't aware that any deal was being negotiated and that it wasn't the way such things should be done. He was basically telling us the deal was off, and we were going to have to do everything by the book, which meant executing the extradition order. Yet again I had to tell Johnny that another door had been slammed shut and he was going to have to wait for the wheels of the legal machine to turn.

'Well,' he said, trying to be philosophical, 'they can't think I'm that big a criminal if they were willing to let me come over as a free man to answer a few questions. They must think there's a possibility they've made a mistake if they're willing to compromise like that. I'll agree to do it anyway, whatever the Foreign Office says. I've got nothing to hide and they've guaranteed I will be treated fairly.'

But now Stephen had changed his mind and said he didn't think it would be a good idea for Johnny to give himself up.

'Don't let him go over unless there is a deal in place,' he advised me.

He suggested to the Moroccans that if they just wanted to ask a few questions, why didn't they come over to Spain and see him there? But they wouldn't agree to that either.

'But if I go of my own free will it will show them I'm innocent,' Johnny protested when I relayed Stephen's opinion. 'If I was a big criminal I wouldn't agree to go like this.'

It didn't seem to matter what Johnny said he was willing to do; the authorities took no notice. We had no idea what they were up to as the time dragged on by, and all we seemed to do was go round and round in circles, our morale occasionally picking up due to some new development, only to be brought back down again when that development came to nothing, like all the others. We talked and talked and talked to everyone and anyone who would listen, until I was fed up with the sound of my own voice, but still I kept on making the calls and telling the story.

We hoped the judges in Spain and Morocco were studying the evidence we had sent through and that soon they would come back and admit they had made a mistake and had cancelled the extradition order. But every day that produced no such news brought the dreaded extradition one day closer.

*

There were so many jobs that had to be done when I was back at home. I had to take care of Johnny's house, which he had left in a state of disrepair, meaning to do all those sorts of jobs when he got back from his wind-surfing holiday in Spain. I had to finish the jobs off in order to find decent new lodgers because the one who had been there had done a runner without paying his rent. It was money we could ill afford to lose as the potential costs of freeing Johnny mounted up ahead of us. If I hadn't been able to find good tenants there wouldn't have been any money coming in to pay the mortgage and Johnny would have lost the house by the time he got back to England.

The pressure of taking care of all these details meant I'd had to drop out of the hairdressing course I had enrolled on to improve my earning power; there just weren't enough hours in the day for me to do everything. Sometimes I would be dashing round the local supermarket getting something for our tea, while talking on the phone to a Member of the European Parliament or someone from an embassy somewhere. At other times I would be racing back and forth to the fax machine in the post office, trying to get documents through to the right places and seeing to my normal family chores. There was never enough time for anything. My family and friends were amazing – at times taking over the running of my house and domestic duties. Without their support it would have been impossible to have functioned as I did.

It was just as bad for Catherine. Because she only had access to email at work, and only worked Monday to Thursday, she would come in on Monday mornings to a pile of angry messages from people wanting to know why she wasn't getting straight back to them with answers to their questions. Her husband, Andrew, was a truck driver so he tended to go to bed quite early and she would go back to making phone calls and writing letters late into the night. She was so exhausted she was falling asleep at her desk some days.

One of my highest priorities was to keep a normal life going for Freya. I wanted her to enjoy her friends' birthdays, Christmas, sleep-overs and all the usual things that little girls do. Just because I was distracted and worried all the time didn't mean she had to suffer. Having Freya there was actually a great help to me because it forced me to think about other things for at least a few hours of every day; otherwise every moment would have been taken up with worrying about Johnny and I probably would have gone mad. It must have been hard for Freya to see all the adults in her life so worried. She must have heard a lot of my phone calls and known how bad things were at times, but she was always very brave and didn't nag me for promises about when Johnny would be back with us. Whenever she asked I always assured her that he would be home soon and she seemed willing to trust me. I just wished I could have been as sure as I sounded to her.

Stephen contacted our local MP, Andrew Turner, to ask for his help in making noises in all the right places. He also lobbied a collection of twelve MEPs, including Caroline Lucas and Peter Skinner, all of whom agreed with him that it was completely unacceptable for Spain to be considering extraditing a fellow European to Morocco, particularly when he could prove his innocence so easily. Under pressure from these politicians, Spain reluctantly agreed that their treaty with Morocco wasn't in line with European rulings, but until the law was changed there was nothing they could do about it. In effect Spain just shrugged their shoulders and walked away. The judge in charge of the case could only go by the law books he had laid out in front of him, and it could be many years before they were changed. Every country in Europe, they argued, still had laws that needed to be brought into line with the European constitution; it was something that would take time. But Johnny's life was ebbing away while they all 'took their time'.

I'd heard so much about how prisoners in places like Morocco could end up being tortured, but everyone we spoke to warned us that bringing up those fears would do us no good. The Moroccan authorities would always deny that such things happened and it would be impossible to make a case. We had to concentrate on points of law, nothing else. It was so frustrating and frightening to find that no matter whom we got on our side, we were still running into brick walls.

Despite all the evidence piling up to the contrary, Inés was still optimistic, assuring us that when the Spanish authorities got round to looking at all the paperwork we were sending through they would see that Johnny was an innocent man. We had the speeding ticket from the police to prove that Johnny had come straight back from Agadir after the delivery and had been hurrying back to work. We had collected references from ex-employers and from friends who had positions of influence on the island and knew Johnny's father. We even sent in pay slips to show that he worked during the summer of 1997 after returning from the delivery, which suggested he wasn't a big-time drug smuggler. But how long would it take them to read it all? Would they do it before the time came for Johnny to be extradited? Did the Spanish care either way?

We really wanted Crewseekers, the internet agency who had advertised the job originally, and the yacht brokers who had sold the boat on behalf of the government, to give us statements explaining how the crew had answered advertisements and had nothing else to do with the boat apart from delivering it, but they wouldn't. They said that because the original captain had dropped out and Johnny had found another one, the job was nothing to do with them any more. They wouldn't help, even though they had been dealing with the Cali Cartel representatives on behalf of the government, albeit unknowingly. The agency mentioned being concerned about 'bad publicity'.

Johnny would never have had anything to do with the cartel if these people hadn't brokered the deal, but they wouldn't put that in writing for us, which must have added to the Moroccans' and Spaniards' suspicions. We tried to get the Ministry of Defence to come forward with a receipt for the sale of the boat, which would show how it had been done in good faith, but no one would respond to our request.

Everything we sent had to be translated into Spanish, which was costing us more money. I was spending endless hours beside the photocopying machine in our local store, but none of it seemed to be doing any good.

A group of us went to London to protest, and we had people sending letters off by the hundreds to the Prime Minister and the Foreign Secretary, to the king of Spain and the king of Morocco, but all our pleas were falling on deaf ears. We set up a 'Free John Packwood' website, with a letter to the Prime Minister for people to download and send.

Catherine and I spent virtually every spare moment we had chasing people up, trying to bring more supporters on side and persuading people to come with us to this meeting or that meeting. Some days it seemed like an almost impossible struggle, and still we didn't seem to be getting any further.

One of our earliest protests was to the offices of the

European Parliament in London, where we met the MEPs Stephen had approached for us. We held a press conference there and Josep Borrell Fontelles, the President of the European Parliament, wrote a letter to the Moroccan government, telling them that he was taking a personal interest in the case. Whenever we heard about things like that our confidence would soar; surely they would listen to people this important? But still it didn't seem to have any effect. Señor Borrell and Peter Skinner MEP talked to the Moroccan Ambassador in Brussels, urging him to consider the huge implications that the case held for the whole marine industry, as well as trade between Morocco and Europe, but he said there was nothing he could do.

'But you are our closest link to Morocco,' Señor Borrell protested. 'That is your job.'

'There must be some reason for the extradition order,' the ambassador shrugged.

'Then show it to me,' Señor Borrell demanded. The ambassador promised he would get back to him, but Señor Borrell never heard anything further.

It occurred to us that Interpol must have a record of their conversation with Johnny seven years ago, and that they would be able to vouch for the fact that they had been satisfied of his innocence. We made contact with them, but they denied ever having talked to him. They said they had no record of any such contact. It was puzzling. Were they lying, or had those two men come down to Southampton unofficially, so no records of the trip were ever made? Or were they up to something else? It was so frustrating to feel like such an outsider, always knocking on the doors of the people who seemed to know what was going on and always being sent away without any clear explanation.

John

When I first heard that the 'paperwork' had been sent over for my extradition, I imagined it would be a great thick document, listing many detailed reasons why it was right that I should be sent to Morocco to face trial. But when Inés eventually showed it to me it was just a simple piece of paper stating little more than the bare facts of my name, age and profession. There was, however, one paragraph that made my blood run cold. In these few words I could see where the whole misunderstanding lay.

The boat named Duanas *had, as its assignment, the transport of six tonnes of cocaine to the south of Spain; that the crew had to offload the narcotics, dumping them near the Moroccan coast because the ship's engine broke down. The ship was under the command of an English crew until it arrived at the port of Agadir … the practical investigation into the case determined the identity of the crew as ... [it listed all our names], all English nationality, implicated and complicit in an international drugs network.*

Anyone reading that muddled paragraph, obviously written by someone who not only didn't speak English as a first language, but also hadn't really understood the story, would be forgiven for thinking that we were the ones sailing the *Duanas* on the night of the drugs bust. There was no indication that we had left the boat ten weeks earlier and that another crew of Panamanians and Colombians had been arrested on board with the drugs months later. The reason they could list our names with such confidence was that we were the only people in the whole episode who had used our real passports – another indication that we had never had anything to hide. Unless we could persuade the authorities to look beyond this misleading paragraph to the evidence we were submitting they would continue to think we were mercenaries working at the dark heart of the drug-smuggling business.

Another complication was that everyone who knew anything about the Moroccan justice system advised me not to claim that I was innocent, as that would imply a fault with their system and would be taken as an insult. That seemed like the ultimate catch-22.

Whenever I had mail at Valdemoro they would call my name out over the tannoy: 'Packwooo!' I would then have to line up at the window with the others while the guards opened the mail, looking for money, and passed it through. Jane would send me 'blue ones' which were air-mail letters I would get within three days, and 'brown ones' which were envelopes full of emails, newspaper cuttings or anything else she thought would cheer me up. By sending this stuff she was letting me know that something was going on out there, that people were still fighting to get me out. I could see that she was making sure no one forgot where I was.

Inés seemed to have changed her battle plan. Whereas she had been very optimistic when we first took her on, certain she would get me off, she was now saying she thought my best hope was the lobbying being done by the MEPs, Fair Trials Abroad and my family. I was begin-ning to wonder what she had done for the £8,000 we had paid her.

'I always thought you would be extradited,' she told me on one of her rare visits. 'Ninety-nine per cent of people in your position are.'

How pointless her job must feel to her, if that was the case, I thought. It seemed I should have been listening to my fellow prisoners from the start. All their predictions were proving to be completely accurate. I guess they were the guys who were the real experts in extradition. It was beginning to look as if there was no way to avoid ending up in a Moroccan jail and my nights were trou-bled with vivid nightmares of what now lay in store. My previous, peaceful life on the island was beginning to seem a very distant memory and, in my lowest moments, I wondered if I would ever get back. Would I ever see my dear old mum again?

Christmas passed in the prison without leaving a single footprint, just one more day, exactly like all the others. It helped in a way because I was missing the family so much that any reminders of the festive season might have been too painful to bear.

CHAPTER FIVE

Jane

Christmas was bad; no one in either of our families felt like getting together for the usual celebrations. We struggled to go through the motions, trying to maintain normality for the children. It was just more time to be endured when people who might help us were away from their desks and their offices were closed. Soon after the holiday Catherine and I both received emails from someone who claimed to be a Moroccan police sergeant involved in Johnny's case. He seemed to know all about it. Reading what he had to say made me feel confused at first and then gradually, as his meaning sunk in, I felt sick.

He said that he wanted to help Johnny get out of jail. He told us that all our telephone calls and letters were being intercepted by Spanish police intelligence officers, and copies were being sent to the police in Morocco. He mentioned one letter in particular that only someone in the prison service could have seen. He warned that if we showed his email to anyone like a lawyer, the police or an MP, Johnny would be affected, and his case would suffer. He threatened that unless we kept quiet Johnny would be sent to a high security wing in a Moroccan prison and would be punished. He said that if we promised to keep it secret, he would write to the Spanish government on behalf of the Moroccan police and tell them that they didn't want Johnny to be extradited any more. He warned that if John ever reached Morocco, he would never be set free because they had other evidence against him.

Even though everything he was saying didn't make complete sense, partly because of his broken English, I felt deeply threatened that someone like this could know so much about us, and could get a message like this into my home. Catherine didn't have a computer at home and was doing everything when she was at work, so she didn't feel quite as invaded. Every time my computer announced I had a new email I felt nauseous. Knowing he, and whoever else he was working with, knew my address made me nervous in the darkest hours of the morning when it was just Freya and me in the house alone, with only Badger for protection. Threatening words from a stranger can have a terrible effect on you when your defences are low and you feel vulnerable and helpless.

Within a few days the 'sergeant' had revealed his true colours and was asking for a payment of 10,000 euros (and another 10,000 euros once Johnny had been released). I was to send the money in cash to Spain via Western Union. Catherine and I didn't know what to do. If the writer of the emails knew so much about our situation, then presumably he was in a position to make Johnny's life worse if we didn't pay up. I knew Johnny was already being victimised in prison and I dreaded making things worse by not cooperating with this man. Maybe he was even genuine and could do something to help stop the extradition. After seeking professional advice, Catherine and I decided that we should pay, and hope for the best. Apparently it was not uncommon for deals to be struck this way and it seemed worth the chance. We took the difficult decision not to tell John, as we had no idea of this person's true identity or to what extent our calls were being monitored.

I seemed to be living in the post office. There were always so many little things to remember. When it was Catherine's or Frances' birthday, I would need to send a card out to Johnny, so he could sign it and send it back to England. When it came to my fortieth birthday, he and Catherine managed to sort me out a bunch of flowers. It was very moving to think that even with all he was going through, he was still taking the trouble to do things like that for me. I liked the idea that we could make him feel that he was still able to participate in normal family things, even at that distance.

Money was disappearing at a frightening rate. I was taking cash into the prison to help Johnny survive, sometimes hiding it in my boots if I was going for a visit, or sending him a photograph of me and Badger, mounted on a card, with some money slipped in between. My second visit to Valdemoro was in February, when there was still snow on the ground, making the place look even more bleak and threatening. Again I was ejected back out into the darkness after visiting time, snow flurrying around my face, stinging my eyes as I waited for yet another taxi. I felt drained and exhausted by the months of worry and struggle.

On my third visit down to Valdemoro, I took a film crew from Meridian Television, our local station, with me. Hugh Kirby, the journalist, had over the months become a friend to me and to John's family. He always seemed to take a personal interest in our plight and we felt we could trust him. It felt good to have their support and to know they would be showing people in England just how serious the situation had become, but it also made it harder for me. They were waiting to film the moment I came out from visiting Johnny. Just a few minutes after saying an emotional goodbye to the man I loved, I had to compose myself and talk to the cameras. It left my head and my feelings spinning. I held on tight, determined not to cry in front of the media. I felt I needed to appear strong and in control, but all I really wanted to do was scream. It was like watching a train crash approaching and not being able to do anything to prevent it.

Andrew Turner, our MP, arranged for us to have a meeting with the Moroccan Ambassador in London. A group of us had already been to the embassy to hand in letters, trying to alert them to the problem, but without any success. The meeting with the ambassador was equally fruitless.

'I am merely a postman,' he kept telling us, in case we thought he actually had the power to change anything. 'Mr Packwood only has to prove his innocence.'

'No,' Catherine reminded him, 'with your new criminal code he's innocent until proven guilty.'

'Yes, yes, of course,' he reassured us, but we could tell that in fact he was right. It was going to be down to Johnny to prove to the Moroccan judge that he'd had nothing to do with the drugs. We knew we could do that, as long as we could just get them to read all the evidence that we were putting together. Now that it looked like he would end up in Morocco we were having everything translated into Arabic as well as Spanish, which meant even more money was seeping away through our fingers. The little bit of capital John had so proudly realised from the sale of his house, and that he had hoped would set him up with a business, had now virtually gone. I had no idea where I would turn if the money finally ran out.

'Any questions that you need to ask me,' the ambassador went on, smiling charmingly, 'I won't be able to answer as I don't know the details of your case. But if you would like to give them to me in writing I will send them to the appropriate people.'

I already knew that was an empty promise, having sent a number of letters to officials in Morocco and never receiving replies.

On another occasion Andrew Turner managed to get us a meeting with the Minister for Europe, Douglas Alexander, in the grandeur of Portcullis House. I went with Andrew Turner, Catherine's husband and Stephen Jakobi. We didn't achieve much; he just told us they were monitoring the case and couldn't interfere in another country's judicial process.

'We are watching the case,' he assured us, but that didn't make me feel any better. Johnny had always told me that he believed the British government would get its citizens out of most difficult situations throughout the world. He had always felt proud to be British when he was travelling. Up until now he had been saying that they would never let an innocent man be sent to Morocco, but now he didn't sound so sure. No one seemed to have the courage to speak up for John. I left feeling very unimpressed.

Frances, worried that she might never see her son again, started talking about going out to visit him in Valdemoro. Having made the trip myself several times I knew it would be impossible. They would often keep us waiting for hours in different stone corridors and waiting rooms around the prison, where there weren't even chairs to sit on. Her hips would never have stood it. Johnny was in agreement that we had to dissuade her, knowing that the sight of her son in such a place would be too upsetting.

Even though Johnny was beginning to think there was a possibility he might have to go to Morocco, I just couldn't bear to picture it happening. I couldn't imagine how we were going to cope. At that stage I was still just fighting to get him back from Spain, trying to convince myself that would be enough. The thought of Morocco made me feel sick with worry. How would he be treated as a westerner in a Muslim jail during such turbulent political times? I couldn't even hear the name without feeling ill.

John

I could tell there was something wrong when I spoke to Jane on the phone, but she kept saying it was nothing. She'd been told by her mystery emailer not to tell me anything, and he had also told her our phone calls were being listened to, but she still wasn't able to disguise the new tone of worry in her voice and for several days I wasted precious minutes from each phone call trying to wheedle the truth out of her. She kept saying she didn't want to talk about it over the phone, but I couldn't bear the agony of waiting until the next visit. I kept on and on at her until eventually she told me about the emails she had been receiving from some police official in Morocco, promising to get the extradition order cancelled in return for some money. I could tell she was frightened by his threats, by how much inside knowledge he seemed to have of the case, and by the fact that he knew where she lived. It did all sound very threatening, but I couldn't help but hold out some hope he might be genuine. Any straw that passed my way I was grabbing at by then.

The idea of yet more money disappearing into the ether, however, was frightening; what would happen when everything I had managed to save up had gone? What would we do then? There was no one else we could turn to for help.

'We could get you moved to another wing for your safety,' Jane suggested once she had told me about the threats.

'No!' I shouted, frightened we would be cut off before I had a chance to tell her that would be the worst thing to happen. Everyone had told me that however bad this wing was, the others were worse. It seemed to me that the emailer held all the cards and we had no choice but to pay him. I agreed with Jane and Catherine's decision, and just prayed that he was genuine in his offer. Discovering that everything I did and said in prison was being reported on to someone else was terrifying. It added yet another layer of fear and paranoia to my daily routine as I tried to find people I could trust to talk to, increasingly aware that probably I could trust no one.

Catherine had sent me forms to fill in to give her power of attorney over my savings so she could access them when funds were needed to fight the campaign. At that moment I didn't care how much it would end up costing me, just as long as I got safely home, although it still made me angry to think I was having to spend my hard-earned life savings just to prove that I was innocent. I had so much time to brood on my situation, my anger kept on bubbling up inside me. I couldn't believe that the British government could sell a military ship direct to the Cali Cartel in Colombia, and that the agency we got the job through could accept the Cali Cartel as clients, without there being any backlash, whereas I could innocently deliver the ship for them and end up accused of being part of their drugs business. The British government was in effect doing business with one of the most notorious drugs cartels in the world and no one was doing anything to help me. The Spanish government could also flaunt the laws of the European Union and I was helpless to appeal. The injustice of it all just kept grinding round and round in my head.

I didn't think Inés had made my case strongly enough. She seemed to be relying on the authorities to make the right decisions without ramming home all the reasons why it was obvious I was innocent. She wasn't making the point that I was in England at the time of the drugs bust, that I had never met any of the people involved, that I had never even visited either Colombia or Las Palmas or Spain before, which was the route the drugs were taking. There was simply nothing to connect me to the crime, apart from the fact that I had once been on the boat. But she didn't make any of those points. It seemed I was being served up on a plate; what had happened to my basic human rights? I could see that her methods might post-pone the moment when I was extradited, but I couldn't see them actually getting me freed. I felt so helpless to do anything to defend myself, not understanding the system or even the language.

The deadlines for my release promised by our Moroccan emailer kept changing, and the emails were making less and less sense with each one. We held onto our hopes for as long as we possibly could, but eventually we had to admit that we had been conned and intimidated out of money we desperately needed. The question was, how had they managed to get so many details about our situation? The only solution we could think of was that someone in the jail had been reading all my letters, listening in to my phone calls and any other information they could find. It seemed it was a highly organised scam, one we would never have fallen for had we not been so desperate and so near to the end of our tethers. This man's dire predictions of what would happen to me once I got to Morocco kept echoing in my mind. Whatever happened, I had to keep fighting the extradition. However bad conditions were in Valdemoro, they would be a great deal worse over there.

I was not amazed when I discovered that we had been duped out of our money, but it was still a disappoint-ment. When you are desperate to believe something you will sometimes turn a blind eye to the obvious. I had seen other inmates scouring the newspapers for hard luck stories and then contacting people on the outside, telling them to go to these people and offer help, and then ripping them off. Just from listening in to conversations I knew that Spain was full of con artists, and a lot of them were in Valdemoro. Why had I not realised that the emails for Jane were just a money-making scam? I guess it was because I wanted them to be genuine and for our mystery Moroccan policeman to prove to be the real thing. After all, the story he was telling was no more outlandish than the reality of what had happened to me. If a man could be arrested for something he didn't do seven years before, and could be held without questioning or charging for months and threatened with extradition, was it not equally possible that a well-aimed bribe could put an end to the whole charade?

Inés explained to me that the Moroccan government now had another thirty days in which to come and pick me up. If they failed to meet that deadline I would be free to leave prison. I had been made too many promises like that to believe it was true. They seemed to be able to make and drop deadlines like that whenever they felt like it. However, I couldn't help praying that maybe this time she was right and they just wouldn't bother to come for me.

Now that the summer had returned the heat was unbearable. During afternoon lock-up, when we were supposed to have our siestas, I would just lie very still in my boxer shorts and sweat like I was in a sauna.

Sometimes I would lie on the concrete floor to try to get cool, my face beside the crack under the door, like a dog trying to pick up any tiny bit of breeze. In the evening, when the air outside cooled, the heat would emerge from the concrete as the humidity would rise and cook us all over again. It was like sitting in a furnace and even in the middle of the night it could be as hot as midday.

Jane

However hard we might still have been hoping for a last minute reprieve, it was looking more and more likely that Johnny was going to end up in a Moroccan jail – a really frightening prospect for all of us. I finally had to accept this as a possibility.

On my final visit to Madrid we both knew this might be the last time we would see each other for a long time. It would be far harder for me to get to see him if he was locked up in Morocco. Even if I managed to make the trip, the authorities might not let us meet. It was not a culture I knew very much about, but I was under the impression that women did not have the same status as they did in Europe. Catherine and I were likely to find our campaign to prove his innocence much harder to fight outside the European Union.

If things continued the way they were going, Johnny might even be found guilty and would then not be back home for ten, twenty or even thirty years. Many of the people he knew would be dead or would have moved on by then. His life would have passed by while he sat in a prison cell. It was a heavy thought to carry as we tried to make the visit as pleasant as possible.

I had decided to try to make the idea of him moving to Morocco as small a leap into the unknown as possible by scouring the internet for any information on the subject. The more we knew what to expect, the better prepared John could be to face it when the time came. I discovered there were websites set up specifically to brief people on what to expect once they got there, written by people who had actually been through the experience, or advised by people who had. I started reading and printing – none of the news was good. One of the website authors I made contact with was someone who had actually served a prison sentence in the country.

'Tell him it will be hard,' he said, 'but he will survive, because people do.'

He also told me that the one prison Johnny did not want to be taken to was Kenitra, because it was notoriously tough and the conditions primitive.

Because Johnny had now been in jail in Spain for nearly a year, I knew there were some people in the Isle of Wight who were beginning to think that there must be something in the charges. Surely, they reasoned, no one would be held that long without a trial – 'no smoke without fire', as they say. I was shocked by how many empty promises I received. They would all pay lip-service to offering their help when they talked to me, but most of them never followed through by actually coming up with anything positive. There were even some men who took the opportunity to try to persuade me I was wasting my time waiting for Johnny to come back, that I should give up on him and go out with them instead. I felt it was hard for Freya too, hearing all the time that her mother's boyfriend was in prison. Eventually people forget that something is a miscarriage of justice, and just remember the fact that a man has been imprisoned for a connection with drug running.

I was also beginning to worry that we still hadn't found the right people at the British end to help Johnny get free. I wasn't the only one in the family to feel that we needed to be more proactive. Jenny, who was the daughter of John's cousin David, had told us about a friend of hers who was a high-profile media lawyer called Jason McCue. When I mentioned it to Stephen Jakobi he tried to reassure me that he was our British lawyer, but somehow we felt something was missing. I knew that Fair Trials Abroad had nearly 400 cases on their books; they were weighed down with work and couldn't hope to give us as much time as we needed. Catherine and I talked it over for hours on the phone, both of us worried that we would end up wasting yet more money and getting no further, but eventually we decided we had no choice but to try. Johnny's savings weren't going to be any use to him if he ended up being locked up for the next twenty years; it was better to use them to try to get him free.

Catherine and I went with Jenny's father, David, to London to meet Jason in his office. Neither of us felt particularly optimistic; it seemed like just one more avenue that would turn out to be a dead end after we had exhausted ourselves exploring it. There had been so many people who had put us in contact with people they said would be able to help, but who turned out to be as powerless as we were. We felt exhausted by the whole process. Catherine was under even more stress than me, having family worries, plus an important job to hold down and Frances to look after until Johnny got back. Frances was living with her at the time, having undergone a hip replacement. We must both have looked wretched, having lost substantial amounts of weight and had a year of anxiety and fear etched into our faces.

Jason's offices at H_2O Law were in Chancery Lane. They were trendy – all glass and leather inside a traditional Victorian building. Everyone seemed very young and energetic, yet laid-back at the same time. When Jason himself came striding out to greet us I was immediately struck by his charisma. As he led us into his office I noticed he wasn't wearing a suit, just a shirt, jeans and boots. He was unshaven and puffing on a large smelly cigar as he listened to our story – not the usual lawyer type.

Despite the bustle of the office going on around us he seemed to be able to give us as much time as we needed, giving the impression that he was actually interested in hearing what had happened. We talked for two-and-a-half hours and I was impressed to find he already knew a lot about the case; someone had briefed him well before we got there. He seemed totally confident and had a quick grasp of the whole situation. He didn't ask any of the dumb questions we had been asked a hundred times before by everyone else we had ever gone to for help. He seemed to understand and be completely certain that he could get Johnny back. In fact he seemed to be champing at the bit to start work on the case. This was not Jason's usual type of case but he was willing to take it on, on merit alone.

By the time we walked out of the office again I felt a massive sense of relief, as if someone had lifted the entire weight of the case off our shoulders. I didn't say anything to Catherine because I wanted to find out how she felt first. I knew she was a much tougher nut to crack than I was. I wasn't sure she would have been impressed by Jason's flamboyance and his tendency to swear at everything. As we came out into the street she looked at me and just quietly said, 'Yeah.'

'Thank God for that,' I said. 'I was worried you wouldn't feel the same way I did.'

We both wished we'd found Jason months earlier, although at that time we had never imagined we would ever need to resort to such drastic measures. If anyone could get Johnny back for us, this was the man.

CHAPTER SIX

John

I was nervous when Jane told me about the flash British lawyer she had found. I was still thinking there was a 50/50 chance that if I got taken to Morocco they would just look at the evidence, realise there had been a mistake and send me straight home. Did I want to spend the last of my savings on yet another lawyer who didn't make any difference? Was it going to be one more person jumping on the bandwagon? On the other hand, what if things continued to go as badly wrong as they had so far?

My cousin, David Packwood, and his wife, Jo, who were Jenny's parents, came out to see me, to try to convince me that hiring Jason would be the right thing to do. I was touched that they made the effort to travel all that way. They said they were surprised how well I looked. Maybe that had something to do with the weight I was losing. I'd gone into prison weighing 13 stone and by then I was down to ten and a half. I know I looked pallid too, from lack of sunlight.

Jane begged me to give Jason a try. 'He wants to come over to Spain to see you,' she said. 'Will you talk to him?'

I could tell it meant a lot to her, and I was anxious to take as much of the weight off her shoulders as possible, so I agreed, even though I was worried about the potential cost of an expensive lawyer coming all the way out to Madrid from London. Jane had told me he was married to journalist and broadcaster Mariella Frostrup and was a friend of the stars, people like George Clooney, Brad Pitt and Hugh Grant. She assured me that once I met him I would feel the same way she did. She was right. He bowled into the prison like a breath of fresh air, apparently completely unintimidated by the whole experience. I could tell immediately that he understood exactly what had happened and to my relief he didn't seem to think there was any reason why he wouldn't be able to fix things. He seemed quite surprised that it had taken us a year to come to him.

'I can get you out of this,' he said at the end of our visit, 'but it will cost you.'

'Whatever it takes, mate,' I said. What use were my savings to me if I was going to be rotting for the rest of my life in a jail cell? I'd made a decision to trust him and put my faith, as well as my savings, in his hands. Jane's judgement had proven sound as usual.

'If you'd come to me a month ago I would have been able to put a stop to this extradition order,' he said, 'but it may be too late for that. If you do end up in Morocco I'll come straight over and kick some arse till I get you out.'

'I haven't got that much money,' I confessed, 'what happens when it runs out?'

'John,' he said, 'I will stick with you to the end, even if I have to do this in my own free time.'

After the meeting I went back to my cell feeling that we finally had someone with us who had the guts to get something done. Stephen had done a great job, but he had so many other cases to worry about that he couldn't risk ruffling too many feathers. There would be no more creeping around trying to be diplomatic, trying not to offend anyone. That hadn't worked and now we needed to start shouting our arguments from the rooftops. Jason was so full-on I did worry that he might end up upsetting the very people we needed to influence, but on balance I thought that was a risk worth taking. Diplomacy had only led to me wasting a year of my life waiting for something to happen. It was time to try something different.

I was also still hoping the Moroccans might never come to get me – that they would simply think I wasn't worth the bother. But on that front my luck had run out. One morning the screws told me they were on their way to pick me up. Swiss Pieter, my lawyer friend, had helped me write my story out in French, so I would be able to show it to any guard or fellow prisoner in Morocco who could read the language. He had also given me his watch as a gesture of friendship. I was deeply touched and wished I had something to value to give him in return.

I had no idea what I was allowed to take with me. I'd heard different stories from everyone I'd talked to. I wanted to take as many belongings as possible because I knew I would be provided with virtually nothing once I got there, and it was going to be a lot harder for Jane to get things to me than it was in Spain. I'd bought myself a Walkman from the prison catalogue to play the tapes Jane had sent me. It had taken six weeks to arrive. The night before I was due to leave I had a chance to call Jane. It felt like the longest five minutes when all I had left to say was 'goodbye'. I packed up all my little luxuries and they escorted me back to *ingresso* for the last time.

The next day I was transported to the cage at the airport, reminding me of where my whole sorry adventure had started. I was left sitting on the stone bunk for six hours until two smartly dressed Moroccan men turned up to fetch me. One was carrying a briefcase, which seemed incongruous somehow, considering how little paperwork it had required to get me extradited. I guess they were policemen having a nice day out, like the two men from Interpol who came down to Southampton to see me.

I was taken out of the cell and asked to sign several

documents – a bit like a car being transferred to a new owner. Someone took my bags and one of the Moroccans put his arm around me, as if to reassure me. He could clearly see I was shaking.

'Okay,' he said. 'You okay now. You don't worry any more.'

It was a shockingly sweet gesture compared to the sort of abruptness I had grown used to in Spain. They both seemed extraordinarily nice men. It was almost as if they actually felt some compassion for me, could imagine how it felt to be in my shoes. I began to wonder if perhaps I was going to be okay now I'd left Valdemoro. If everyone in Morocco was as understanding and sincere as these two, perhaps they would see how worried I was and would help me out. They each took hold of one of my hands and escorted me out to a car. They were going to drive me out to the plane, a commercial flight waiting on the tarmac.

When we reached the edge of the runway they parked and went up into the plane to find out where we were going to be sitting, leaving me alone and uncuffed in the car. They had even left the keys in the ignition and the engine running. For a few seconds I contemplated jumping into the front seat and driving off, but luckily I stopped myself before the fantasy turned into a fiasco. Then I started imagining things like Jason coming charging over the horizon with Brad Pitt and George Clooney, heavily armed to spring me loose just in the nick of time.

Even if I had made a bid for freedom, where would I have gone to? I didn't have a passport so I wouldn't have been able to get out of the country, even if they hadn't been on the lookout for me. I probably wouldn't even have been able to get off the tarmac without being shot. I stayed where I was and waited to see what would happen next, numb and dazed by the way my life was changing without any input from me.

The Moroccan men came back down the steps to fetch me, smiling and beckoning as if we were all off on a holiday together. As I climbed out of the car I wondered how many years it would be before I was back on European soil.

They insisted on holding my hands as we walked down the aisle to the back of the cabin, our progress followed by every pair of eyes in the plane. I felt embarrassed to be seen holding hands with two grown men, but despite the strange looks, it was better than being cuffed. I felt slightly reassured by their gentleness after the months of casual brutality I had witnessed and experienced in Madrid. I began to wonder if it had been wise to fight so hard against extradition. If I had agreed to go a year before maybe I would already be back in England.

They led me to a set of three seats and indicated I should sit in between them. One of them kept his hand on my knee throughout the flight, as if to keep me calm and allay any fears the flight might cause me.

A police van waited on the tarmac at Casablanca, parked up in the baking sun, containing uniformed policemen. I was led across to them, handcuffed and bundled inside. It seemed the flight had been a surreal interlude and it was now back to business as usual. With a sinking heart I realised that I had lost my two kindly guardians and was back in the prison system. My travelling companions objected when their uniformed colleagues got out the cuffs, assuring them it wasn't necessary, that I wasn't a risk. But they took no notice – rules are rules I suppose, and maybe they were not senior enough to be able to bend them with impunity. They didn't treat me badly, but there were no more of the reassurances I had received on the way over.

We drove for a day, all the way to Rabat and then on to Kenitra. They took me first to the courthouse, where I waited two hours in a cell before being taken in for processing. I was now the first Briton ever to have been extradited to Morocco. My only crime had been to be naïve and not to have asked enough questions before accepting a job.

'I need my lawyer,' I said, to anyone who would listen, giving them Ben's telephone number, but they all brushed my pleas aside as if I was just being foolish and causing trouble unnecessarily. I showed them Pieter's declaration in French, but they refused to take any notice. I felt like a small child trying to catch the attention of busy, impatient grown-ups. All they wanted at this stage was my name and my date of birth in order to send me on the next leg of my journey to the remand prison.

I felt very small and a million miles from home. I feared I was about to disappear completely off the radar screens of everyone in Britain who might want to help me, swallowed up by a huge, mysterious, medieval prison system that was unlike anything I could understand.

Jane

Having been dealing with the Spanish prison system for a year now, we had got to know our way around the rules and regulations. Our relationship with the embassy officials in London and Madrid had developed to the degree that we were now on first-name terms and felt they empathised with us, often trying over and above the call of duty to help us with our endless requests for information on legal and welfare matters. We had learnt, for instance, how to get money to Johnny and roughly when it would arrive. We knew what he needed in order to get food; we understood the way things were done, as much as it was possible to do so. Now, as he disappeared from Europe, we had to start again finding our way around a whole new system and new officials – like kids arriving at a new school.

The news of John's extradition was met with a mixture of fear and an odd sense of relief. We knew that this was the beginning of the end, whichever way it turned out. Morocco was the place where the story had started and only there, it appeared, could it end.

Some things were becoming easier. Now we had Jason on our team, people in England seemed to be taking more notice of us. Interest from the media had always come in waves, but Jason seemed able to whip up a storm at a moment's notice. Whenever there was a development the press would be back outside the house with their tape recorders and notepads out, and then it would all go quiet again for a while, particularly at weekends when it was impossible to get any responses out of anyone official. Catherine and I always hated the weekends, when everyone in the world was away from their desks and it was impossible to achieve anything. If ever something went wrong it always happened at the end of the week. We would always say, 'Wait till Monday, then things will happen,' because that seemed to be the pattern.

Sometimes Catherine and I found it hard to support each other through the down patches, because we were always going through them at the same time. Having hardly known one another at the beginning of the year, we had now been through virtually every emotion together and our moods would swing between euphoric optimism and deepest despair. Jason's mood, however, never varied from bullish and he was always able to lift our spirits when they were at their lowest ebb and everything seemed hopeless.

It was always hard to find the right phrases to use to keep Johnny feeling positive. I would hear myself dishing out clichés over the phone like 'stay strong', which sounded so meaningless in the circumstances, particularly as he didn't have any option. Jason didn't bother with any of that, he just charged ahead, as if working on the assumption that he was going to have everything fixed in no time and we just had to be patient till then.

Our phone calls from Johnny in Valdemoro were so rushed they often ended badly. Catherine or I would sometimes tell him something that would panic him and he would shout at us. When Catherine told him we had decided to go for maximum publicity now, for instance, he yelled at her not to do it, worried that the Moroccans would start to think he was more important than he was. The phone line was cut at that point, leaving us not knowing what to do for the best and him worrying that we might be doing something that would antagonise the Moroccans and endanger him once he got to their country. If we'd had longer to talk things through we could have put his mind at rest more often. He would have so much time alone with his thoughts he would sometimes lose all perspective. He would often resort to swearing down the line in his frustration, apologising all the time for taking it out on me. I didn't mind if he swore, I didn't take it personally. I knew he had to let it out to someone and he couldn't shout at other prisoners. Catherine took a fair amount of abuse down the phone as well and she was starting to give as good as she got, having never sworn much before. We were all dealing with so much anger all the time.

At the same time we were continually grasping at straws, trying to find good news to tell him and feeling disappointed when it failed to please him. We often had to start phone calls apologising for whatever had gone wrong during the last one.

However bad the previous year had been, we had grown used to the routine of the calls and the trips and sending of letters and money. We had no idea how to start establishing a similar supply line of hope and information to him in Morocco.

John

Kenitra was the rural area where the cocaine haul had washed up on the beach from the *Duanas* all those years ago. The prison there was built at the beginning of the nineteenth century by the colonial French. Jane had been told it was the worst prison in Morocco to end up in and as such, the one I most wanted to avoid. The moment I realised that was where we were headed, I just wanted to die rather than face whatever unknown horrors lay ahead.

After a year of having my expectations built up only to be knocked back down, I was beginning to doubt I would ever be a free man again. If no one had been able to save me in Spain, what hope did I have now, in a Muslim country, especially at a time when the West were holding many of their citizens around the world in prisons without trial? I was imagining the rough time my fellow inmates would give me as the police van turned up a bumpy unmade road towards the gates.

Still handcuffed, I was led into a small office, which looked like a set from a pre-war movie, with old-fashioned typewriters and no sign of any modern technology. It was hot and airless and flies settled on the sweat of my forehead. Despite the primitive surroundings, the atmosphere was gentler than in the many Spanish *ingressos* I had been through. There was no strip-searching. I was just told to sit on a seat while they processed me, writing down all the information I gave them. No one seemed to speak any English so it all took a long time, but they spoke politely and treated me with dignity. They kept my possessions to sort through and search, and helped themselves to anything they fancied before passing them on to me.

Eventually I was escorted into the main prison through gates in a wall of bars. A man was hanging by his wrists from the bars beside the gate, his arms twisted behind his back, his feet swinging a metre above the floor, blood running down his arms from where the cuffs had cut into his wrists, puddling on the floor below. There were prisoners coming and going all around the area, but all of them averted their eyes from their unfortunate colleague, apparently wanting to protect his dignity and not wanting to give the guards the satisfaction of knowing they had seen him.

I was soon to learn there was always someone strung up on the bars as an example to the rest of us; usually it seemed to be a young boy who had been too cheeky to a guard during the day and had been pulled from his cell in the night to be taught a lesson. They would be stood on a stool and their wrists chained to the rails above their heads. The stool would then be kicked away and they would be left dangling, crucified and bleeding. If they looked like they were going to pass out, the guards would throw water over them to bring them round.

The nights were always filled with the screams of prisoners having the soles of their feet beaten. A lot of the boys would cut themselves in desperate cries for help, and their arms were covered in scars. It seemed to me that a lot of these inmates should have been in mental hospitals, not prison. Most nights, at about three in the morning, someone would be dragged off.

Out of a population of around 30 million in Morocco, very nearly half are under fifteen. Less than half the population are able to read or write. Many of the boys and men who were part of this underclass lived most of their lives in prisons of one sort or another.

I was escorted to a cell, which can't have been more than about 20 square metres, containing forty-six other men. There were no windows. The only natural light came from slits high up in the walls, about 15 feet above our heads, dusty shafts criss-crossing the ceiling but never penetrating the gloom below. A cable looped around the room to power the lone electric light bulb that dangled from the ceiling. Another wire had been splinted on to power a cooking ring. Washing hung from lines everywhere, like in a photo of some over-crowded city ghetto from one of the crueller periods of history. There was a hole in the floor in the corner of the room, which served as a lavatory and for any other waste products like left-over food. There was a single tap above it for washing. I wondered what in God's name I would do if I caught a stomach bug. In the end, the diet had the opposite effect on me and I didn't crap at all for the first six days — a situation that eventually became even more worrying. In a prison cell with nothing to do, you have a lot of time to worry about things like a pain in your tooth or the lack of movement in your bowels. It's impossible to take your mind off anything that is worrying you.

There was no furniture in the cell. All forty-seven of us had to live, eat and sleep on the floor, wherever we could find a space. A newcomer like me would start with a place in the centre of the cell. Those who had been there a long time had worked their way to the walls and, eventually, if they were lucky and respected by the oth-ers, to a corner. Only then did they have any support for their aching backs during the long hours of sitting.

The stench of hot, unwashed bodies mingled with the aromas of food and faeces. It was hard to breathe the thick, smoky air without gagging. All I could think was that this had to be the most horrible place on earth for any living thing to be.

At first I could see no space to sit and so just stood among the sea of bodies, waiting to see what would happen next. Every pair of eyes in the room was staring at me, but no one said anything. After what seemed like an age a man stepped out of the crowd, came over to me and tried to communicate.

'You English?'

'Yes.'

'Ah, English!'

He grinned, as if genuinely pleased to meet me. Introductions were made, and I began to understand that each cell had a boss, who would decide eventually where I was to sleep. This boss was a big, fat, arrogant man, eager to exert his power over the others and to show it off to me. That first night there was no space for me to lie down and I slept on top of other men. I was surprised how little they complained at having a foreign man forced into their already cramped space. I didn't sleep anyway, constantly distracted by the movements of the rats that ran around the edges of the room, and the relentless bombing attacks from mosquitoes. There was always someone moving around, using the tap or saying their prayers. Outside the cell there always seemed to be someone screaming and the sound of beatings. The guards' dogs were on the flat roof above and kept barking at every movement and sound they heard through the ventilation holes to the cells. It sounded like there was a pack of them.

As well as rats and mosquitoes there were also cock-roaches far bigger than the ones I'd hunted down in the cells in Spain. I soon learned that you shouldn't squash them because if you did their eggs would squirt every-where, spreading the problem. In the coming weeks I would often wake in the night from a shallow sleep to find one of them in my hair. Desperate to get rid of them I would snatch at them, often leaving the legs behind in the process. The inmates did try hard to keep the floor clean and there didn't seem to be the dust there had been in Spain, just years of ground-in filth.

In the morning the boss woke everyone up and gave them all their orders; some were told to cook, others to wash. I was apparently spared any chores, being the new boy in the room, even though I would have liked to have something to do other than sit and stare into space. There was no privacy, all our ablutions having to take place in front of our cell-mates. The others all wore full-length shirts, so they were able to squat over the hole in the floor without losing too much of their dignity. I, howev-er, had to fight my way out of my jeans and then balance precariously while trying to relieve myself. There was a bucket for us all to wash ourselves afterwards, always using our left hands, so our right hands would be clean for eating. All my cell-mates used their left hands for cleaning their backsides – the same hands they also used when they patted my face all day long. The floor was always swimming with water in that corner of the room.

Nakedness is strictly taboo in Morocco, even when it is just men, so I had to be very careful not to expose myself and cause terrible offence.

I had kept my toothbrush in my pocket, so the guards hadn't deprived me of it. Each day I would make a ritual of cleaning my teeth over the hole, trying not to look down at the effluent swilling around in the current from the running tap. I had to spit into it without breathing in and inhaling the stench. No one else bothered to clean their teeth – most of them had rotted or fallen out leaving mouths full of foul-smelling gums.

The atmosphere among the inmates was different from the Spanish jails. There was none of the struggling for position and dominance; everyone in this cell was so deep in trouble they had nothing to gain from bullying cell-mates. They had everything to gain from cooperating and trying to make life as bearable as possible. At every hour of the day and night they seemed to be praying, loudly reciting the Koran, and I envied them their faith as I sat with the rats, watching them. By this stage I had no faith left in anything, or in anyone apart from my loved ones, and I wasn't even sure if there was anything they could do for me now I was here. I felt like I had moved into another world, one cut off from everything I had ever known, where I knew none of the rules and had none of the language skills needed to find out. I actually felt nostalgic for the luxury of my various cells in Valdemoro.

The guards gave me back my wash things, but nothing else that had come with me from Spain. They kept the little shaving mirror I had managed to procure, and the pack of cards, which I used to play patience with, distracting myself for hours on end. For some reason they had let me keep Pieter's watch, but once I was in the cell I kept it hidden away, partly as I found it impossible to resist looking at it every five minutes, constantly feeling depressed by how slowly the hands were turning.

'Telephone call?' I asked the guards, hopefully on the first day.

'No,' they shook their heads. 'No telephone calls.'

I felt totally isolated and alone. I was later told that if I wanted to make phone calls I needed to write to the judge in Kenitra for permission, in Arabic. In a hopeful moment I thought I had found a man who could read English and write Arabic, but it turned out to be a false promise. I did eventually manage to write anyway, listing the numbers in England that I would be wanting to call, but the permission never came so I can't have got the words right.

Later in the first day Ben, my new Moroccan lawyer, came to visit me and I was taken to the governor's little office to meet him. The sight of a friendly face released the tension, allowing me to break down and cry for the first time since arriving. The more I tried to hold the tears back the more I felt myself welling up, embarrassed to let myself down under the gaze of the guards. I'm sure they'd seen it a thousand times before.

EXTRADITED!

To my surprise my fears about hostility from the other prisoners proved ill-founded. They were all very friendly, treating me as something of a novelty since I seemed to be the only European among the 2,000 prisoners in the jail. Forty-six pairs of eyes followed me everywhere, but without any hatred in them. I can't believe that a Muslim who didn't speak English would receive anything like such a generous and respectful welcome in any prison in Britain.

The following day I was moved to another cell, where there was more space – only twenty-eight fellow prisoners in the room instead of forty-six, making the air seem more breathable. On my way there I noticed two more young men hanging from the gates. It must have been their screams that had disturbed my sleep the night before. Both of them looked as if they had passed out and a guard was slapping one of them about the face and shouting at him to wake up. I wanted to ask someone why they were being punished but I noticed none of the inmates were looking at them or showing any reaction at all. They wouldn't have wanted to give the guards the satisfaction.

My new home was one of the richer cells, where prisoners were cooking better food and didn't have to rely on the prison slops, which the guards would bring round once a day. The soup was dragged down the hall in a massive pot to a chorus of raised voices as hundreds of inmates asked for favours from the guards, like taking something from one cell to another. Anyone who needed the food would hold out a plastic bowl to have it ladled in.

Some of the poorer inmates would survive by washing clothes for the more affluent prisoners. I preferred to do my own laundry. Scrubbing and wringing out were the only exercise I ever got and I wanted to keep at least a few of my muscles from wasting away.

Many of the more desperate prisoners from the poorer cells seemed to me as if they should be in mental homes rather than jail; lost souls wandering around in permanent states of confusion or mania, constantly shouting to themselves or exercising a variety of repetitive physical tics and jerks as they went about their business. Maybe years of incarceration had driven them mad, or maybe they had just failed to fit into the outside world and a prison cell was the only place left for them to live out their years. Whatever the reason for their presence, arriving among them was like descending into hell.

When the guards pointed out my new cell to me I went straight in and sat down on a piece of empty floor, grateful for the space after the last one, not realising that I was supposed to greet the cell boss before doing anything else. The cell bosses controlled everything and you had to ask their permission before doing anything: washing, sleeping, shitting, eating. The boss of this cell was not happy with my careless breach of protocol and snapped something contemptuous and aggressive. I might not have understood the words, but I got the message.

As soon as I realised my mistake I sprang back to my feet and apologised. Graciously nodding his forgiveness, he greeted me formally, kissing me four times. He was well over 6 feet tall, towering over the rest of us, which seemed to give him a natural authority. Whenever he walked out onto the wing he would have his head held high and everyone moved to one side, bowing their heads and greeting him with respect. Even the guards would give him the same four-kiss salute he had honoured me with on arrival.

Each cell had its own boss, but he appeared to be one of the 'bosses among bosses'. No one seemed to want to give him any trouble, so I decided to stay as close to him as possible since he seemed to like me and be willing to offer me his protection. If a squabble flared up in the heat of the moment, he would always remain patient and cool-headed, separating the combatants and sitting them down at opposite ends of the cell, like naughty school children, until they had calmed down.

My new cell-mates were even friendlier than the previous ones, apparently desperate to make me feel at home in their world, almost like a welcomed guest. Part of me was relaxing and allowing the fear to wane, but I was still on my guard, unsure what was happening around me, or what the etiquette might be in different situations. I didn't want to cause offence to anyone by accident. I knew that no one there believed in my innocence, so no doubt part of the respect came from them assuming I was a member of the Cali Cartel. Even the guards were treating me as someone special, but perhaps that was just because I was foreign and different and they weren't sure what to do with me.

'How old are you?' people kept asking me, in a mixture of broken English and sign language.

'Forty-three,' I confessed.

'No!' they would exclaim. 'You look only twenty-five.'

It dawned on me that they had all probably been prematurely aged by the harshness of their lives both inside and outside the jail. It was possible they were all younger than me, despite their scarred, leathery faces, lack of teeth and scrawny frames.

Everybody seemed to want to shake hands with me, some of them several times a day, which was very reassuring, but quite wearing when they were constantly coming by and wanting to reconnect. No one else seemed bothered about washing their hands, so I was left feeling equally dirty, particularly when there was no water for me to wash myself regularly. I didn't like to rub my face or eyes if they itched for fear of passing on infections.

Moroccan prisoners seemed much more accepting of their situation than the Spaniards, and generally far more philosophical about the blows that life dealt them. If the water went off they would exist on whatever they had

managed to get into bottles the night before. If the elec-
tricity went off they would wait patiently in the
blackness, unable to walk about for fear of treading on
others, until it was restored. There was none of the angry
banging or the shouting. It was as if they accepted their
fate as somehow inevitable – the will of Allah, perhaps.

There was an electric coil in the cell, which the
inmates used night and day to boil water and cook on,
since the slops that the prison officers brought round
each day were not enough to keep a man alive. Friends
and families would bring food in on visits and the boss
would decide how it would be distributed among us. He
decided who did the cooking, too.

Everyone wanted to have a job, just to alleviate the
boredom, and they would deliberately make the jobs last
as long as possible. I didn't understand that at first and
tried to show one of my cell-mates a quicker way to peel
hard-boiled eggs by holding them in the water, but he
didn't want to know. He wanted to pass as many hours
as possible fiddling with little bits of shell. They also spent
a lot of time noisily slurping up cups of tea, a sound that
eventually starts to drive you mad when it's happening all
around you all day long. It was almost as if they were in
competition to see who could be the loudest.

They cooked in one big pot containing different
levels: meat on one, vegetables on another and rice or
potatoes on another, like a steamer. That way they were
able to produce a whole meal at the same time, mostly

rice and potatoes, bread and sauces and occasionally a
chicken. Once a meal was cooked it would be heaped
onto big plates and everyone would share it, sitting
around on the floor on plastic mats. Now and then
there would be a delicacy, such as sheep or goat's eye-
balls, which the boss would present to me for all to
see and I would have to swallow it in order to show
my gratitude.

'Hey,' they grinned, 'Mr John, nice, eh?'

I'm sure they knew how hard it was for me and
enjoyed the teasing. The first time I swallowed one in
one go and it wasn't as unpleasant an experience as I had
expected. From then on I would bite into them, feeling
them pop in my mouth before swallowing.

Everyone was always meticulously polite and nobody
grabbed more than their fair share, making sure 'Mr
John' got the choicest helpings, as if I was an honoured
guest at a family gathering. All the time I was eating gin-
gerly on one side of my mouth, terrified to bite on the
side where the cap had come off in Valdemoro. I could
see from looking at the mouths of my fellow prisoners
that there wasn't any dentistry going on.

They never wasted anything. If someone provided a
goat's trotter, for instance, the boss would rip every last
shred of meat off it, having burned off the hair, stinking
out the cell for the next six hours, and share it round.

Occasionally there would be a scrawny chicken sup-
plied. The boss would rip it to pieces with his hands and

pass it around to people he favoured. I was always given a nice piece, but there were some people in the cell who were not approved of and would be left out. I was never left hungry and found I hardly needed any food since I was taking no exercise. I felt guilty about always accepting their food as I had no way of repaying them, since I wasn't getting any supplies brought in to me.

During the month of Ramadan, which started soon after I arrived with a night of singing and dancing around, everyone became as excited as Christian children become on Christmas Day. There was no eating or smoking allowed until 6.30 pm. Once the sun had gone down everyone would light up at once and the whole room would be a cloud of cigarette smoke.

Many of my cell-mates would manage to sleep through the day during Ramadan, with their sheets pulled up over their faces like corpses, waking up at 6.30 pm for their breakfast. I never managed to do that because of all the activity going on around me, and the days seemed even longer without the cooking going on. They would become equally joyful and excited on the last night of the festival.

Tempers frayed particularly badly during the day because people were without food or cigarettes and there would always be fighting breaking out and raised voices. The rows would die away as quickly as they flared up; as soon as they had lit up and had something to eat they would all be sitting with their arms round one another again, the best of friends. Everyone was very physical, often shaving one another very lovingly since there were no mirrors. They would pass the hours by grooming and picking at one another like a pack of monkeys. We would all leave our flip-flops by the door in an attempt to keep the mats a little cleaner and when they stood up in a line together, praying, they would all cross their bare feet over one another, just taking comfort from physical contact with a friend.

There were other water taps outside the cells on the wing, where some people would go to wash during the hours when the doors were unlocked. They would often wash one another, completely unselfconsciously. One heavily scarred man, called The Bull, offered to wash me, but I insisted I was okay. He was very persistent and I wished sometimes they were a little less friendly. It was a kind gesture but I felt overwhelmed, threatened and embarrassed. It was too big a culture leap from the very British way in which I had been brought up. Even the guards would walk around arm in arm.

I didn't step outside the cell very often, even though the doors were opened for two hours a day for over a thousand of us to go out into the corridors and courtyard. It was so crowded at those times it was hard to make headway through the mass of bodies. It was like pushing your way through a backstreet bazaar as they all arranged their drugs, food and fags deals. It all seemed too dangerous and depressing and I would be besieged by beggars, who assumed that because I was European I could give them whatever they asked for. It would have been nice to have been able to go for a walk without the constant battling against the tide. There were too many crazy people who should have been in institutions, too much noise and too much heat. I preferred the safety and relative calm of the cell.

The heat would rise through the day and once they started cooking and smoking it would become unbearable. I didn't want to be touching anyone, I wanted to get as much air circulating around my skin as possible. Sometimes I would be sitting down on the floor and someone would just plonk their bum down on my feet, a bit like Badger would when she was craving attention at home, while two others would sit either side, rubbing against me, while my back was leaning against someone else's. I felt hemmed in all the time, always hot, always uncomfortable, trying to disappear inside myself. Having hidden Pieter's watch away I soon had no idea what time of day it was. I just slept when I could, when the itching from flea and mosquito bites allowed it. I had no idea how long it was going to go on.

Jane had made contact with a truck driver on the internet who had endured nine years in a Moroccan jail. I wasn't sure I would be able to hold onto my sanity for that long. Both his parents had died by the time he came out. He told Jane that for the first five years he had fought to be heard, gone on hunger strike, done everything he could, but in the end he realised it was futile and he just became resigned to his fate, like the Moroccans I was now among, just concentrating on surviving from hour to hour.

There was a small television in the corner of the cell, hardly visible and with an awful picture, showing the Liverpool v Chelsea UEFA Champions League match, reminding me that it had been a year since I had watched Liverpool in the same competition when I was in Spain. I couldn't believe it, but I actually missed being in Spain. I missed Pieter, evening tea, 1 per cent beer, my adjustable lamp, the walks to the shop, the occasional showers, the mail and phone calls and, most of all, the visits from Jane. It had seemed like hell at the time, but looking back now it seemed more like paradise. I now had no pictures of my family on the wall and no mirror to shave in. Instead I just had many more cockroaches and a lot more filth to deal with.

In this second cell at least there was room for us all to sleep in lines on the concrete floor. We would lie top to toe, not unlike a row of corpses with our arms crossed over our chests and no room to curl up. Although it was bad having to sleep with your nose next to someone's feet, it was worse when you were able to smell their breath and feel its heat on your face.

There were still people walking over me as I tried to escape into sleep. With only a blanket between me and the concrete, my back ached continually and there was no position I could get into that would ease the pain. I never slept for more than three or four hours at a time, and I would nod off at all times of the day, because there was nothing to do but sit and stare at the scenes going on around me. The television was on twenty-four hours a day, always jabbering away in Arabic. Whenever the men had discussions they always sounded like shouting matches, and it was the same in the incessant soap operas that played out on the screen, the actors always shouting and gesticulating at one another. All the programmes looked like home-made fictional versions of what was happening all around me all the time. Every few minutes one of my cell-mates would jump up and start accusing his neighbour of something. The rows seldom went beyond shouting – there just wasn't the room for physical violence in the cell.

The television was our only way of seeing into the outside world, but I found myself noticing things I would never normally have seen. Watching two young lovers walking along an idyllic beach in an advert, the only thing I could focus on was the sun loungers, with cushions that looked so inviting when every exhausted muscle in my body was aching. Sometimes they would show an American film, but whenever it came close to a man and woman kissing or touching there would be a sudden jump cut to the next scene, often disrupting the flow quite comically.

The tap in the cell didn't always work but everyone still needed to cook, wash clothes and wash themselves. Sometimes the water would be off for a whole day and I would have to wait as much as thirty-six hours for a wash. If it happened to come on in the middle of the night everyone would immediately wake up and take turns washing, cleaning their clothes and filling water butts before it went off again. It was frightening to be at the mercy of one tap. What would happen if it just didn't come back on again?

On good days I would keep a flannel with me, wetting it under the tap every fifteen minutes or so to wipe away the sweat. The moisture would attract the flies, but it was too hot to cover up with a sheet so there was no escaping them. I hadn't seen daylight since being brought into the prison; the French colonialists who built the place obviously didn't think that prisoners needed windows. The cells felt like medieval dungeons.

During the day I would spend hours watching passing insects, particularly as they settled in clouds on the uncovered food we would soon be eating. Sometimes I would lie on my back, watching them congregate on the ceiling above me, and wondering where their shit was landing.

It amazed me how I could brush a fly off my arm and then watch it circling the cell for a minute before coming back and landing on exactly the same place.

What was it that was so attractive about that particular patch of my arm that would make it want to pass all the other smelly, sweaty bits of skin on offer? Thinking about something like that could pass several minutes of a long day.

I had started to develop raw-looking sores on my legs from where I had scratched endless flea bites. The wounds were starting to fester.

With a mixture of broken English and sign language I managed to tell my cell-mates why I was in prison. Everyone in Kenitra had heard of the 6-ton cocaine haul on the *Duanas* as it was the biggest in Moroccan history, and I could see they thought I was part of the Cali organisation, which gained me some respect. They told me stories of how much of the coke had been swept up onto the beaches. It was obviously a story that had passed into local folklore, which went some of the way to explaining why the politicians were so keen to find as many people as possible to pin it on. Not content with the arrests they had made on the boat, or the contacts that those men gave them, they wanted to sweep me up in the net as well. I guess an Englishman thought to be supplying gun boats to a drugs cartel sounded like a prize catch, as long as they could go on ignoring the evidence that proved my innocence.

The men in the prison obviously all knew the details of the case from the Moroccan newspapers and I wished I could communicate with them so I could ask them questions and get some answers that might help us to build on my case. I was told some of the smugglers who had been caught on the *Duanas* had actually served time in this jail. I was even shown a blanket that one of them had left behind.

Everyone warned me that the judge in the Kenitra was a 'hard man'; it seemed I couldn't expect any leniency. In my more optimistic moments I still clung to the promise that the Moroccan justice system was a fair one, and that once they looked at the facts of the case they would see I was innocent. But how long would it be before someone actually looked at the evidence? How many more people did we have to try to reach just to get me a fair hearing? It was a year since I had been arrested and I still hadn't even been questioned.

Because Kenitra was still in the Dark Ages there were no mechanisms for blocking mobile phone calls. One of my cell-mates, Said, was a political prisoner who had a mobile and he readily let me use it when the boss told him to. As I got to know him better I discovered he had been in jail for seven years and hadn't even been charged yet. He had no idea how much longer he was going to be there, or even if he would ever stand trial, but still he managed to be incredibly good-natured and absolutely refused to accept anything in payment for the phone calls. Such sudden acts of selfless kindness were always shocking. I would phone Jane, letting it ring three times before ringing off, and she knew the number and could phone me back. Once I was making calls again, I still kept sending letters to the prison authorities, begging to use the prison phone. This was partly to avert the guards' suspicions — if they had realised we had a mobile in the cell there would have been a lot of beatings.

Finally I was brought some food by the Vice Consul at the British Embassy, Anne-Marie. She was an English-speaking woman married to a Moroccan. I happily handed the food over to the boss and he arranged for it to be cooked up and shared round. That was fine by me as I was feeling guilty about eating their food without repaying them, and I wasn't sure how to cook most of it anyway. Every time I left the cell for any reason, like a visit, I was body searched and the guards would take any cigarettes they found for themselves. They always gripped my bollocks as if I might be hiding something down there.

The guards were always asking the prisoners for food, drinks, money and cigarettes. Our cell seemed to be the one that attracted them the most, possibly because we were the richest. I knew I was lucky compared with people in some of the other cells. Our boss was a good man and we got a fair amount of food brought in. One day one of the wives brought in a massive bowl of couscous, which was divided up onto five big plates and handed round the cell to five different groups. But then three screws arrived and bullied their way in to help themselves. I suspect some of the people in our cell, particularly Said, were a lot wealthier than the guards themselves. About five men in our cell had nothing brought in to them and relied completely on the generosity of the boss.

He was particularly generous towards me. Not only did he not ask me to do any of the daily chores, which I would have been quite happy to do, he even invited me to sit in his spot in the cell when he went out onto the wing. I felt like I was being asked to keep his throne warm, even though it was still just blankets on the floor. I was worried that this favouritism might annoy the others, but they seemed to accept it quite happily. I felt like a mini boss myself, but maybe he could just see that I was very scared and was putting me in a safe place while he was not around to protect me personally. There was a lot of violence on the wing and sitting in his place did make me feel safer. One day he went to court and was gone all day, but I never moved from the safety of his mat, like an obedient dog that'd been ordered to 'sit' and 'stay'. He came back with the news that he was going to have to spend another eight years in the shit hole, having been there for three years already. I never found out what he had done to be given such a long sentence.

One night, as I was drifting in and out of sleep, I had a dream in which a friend of mine proved to me the power of positive thinking. If I willed something to happen, it actually did happen. Coming back to consciousness I was blearily aware that the dogs were barking again on the roof. Concentrating my mind, I willed them to stop, knowing that once they started they usually went on for hours. To my amazement they suddenly fell silent. I was now more awake and realised the man snoring next to me was the next problem. Focusing hard, I willed him to be silent, and strangely enough he was.

As I drifted back to sleep I kept repeating to myself, 'Jason will soon get me out. Jason will soon get me out.'

There were several occasions when I was taken to a court, transported in a van filled with as many people as possible. The guards would keep pushing bodies in until there wasn't a spare inch left. I would have one man on my lap, another on my shoulders, crushing me into the floor, and still they would keep pushing in more. The vans were always weighed down on their axles, crashing painfully through every pothole.

I wasn't allowed to have a British lawyer acting for me directly, and had to do everything through Ben, but such rules did not deter Jason. I don't know how he managed it, but he arrived in Kenitra to see me and assured me he would have me out within a few days. His confidence was so different from everyone else in the legal and diplomatic worlds that I couldn't help but be swept along on his wave of optimism.

'They're taking you for a hearing,' he said, 'the judge will look at the evidence and kick it out. You'll be coming back to England with me.'

He told me he'd had dinner with the Moroccan Minister for Justice the night before and had been assured that everything would be okay.

'He said to leave it to him to sort out,' he said with the air of a man who had just solved all my problems in one go.

Maybe, I thought, there was something in this 'power of positive thinking' business. I should have known better.

Jane

Once I discovered that Johnny had access to a mobile phone I started investigating the market and discovered a way of getting the tariff for calls down as low as possible. This was our new lifeline, but we were also running out of money and had to save it wherever we could.

Every evening we would talk for half an hour. It cost around £30 but it was an incredible luxury after a year of grabbing five-minute calls whenever we could. It actually gave us a chance to say how much we were missing one another. There had never been any time for the little things when we had so many practical matters to cram into such short calls.

It was hard to hear his voice coming from a place that I could only imagine from movies I'd seen and articles I'd read. Often I would be able to hear the screams of prisoners being beaten in the background as we talked. On one phone call I managed to get Hugh Kirby, the television journalist from Meridian, to record an interview with Johnny. I wanted as much publicity as possible. I wanted people to be able to hear how brave and stoic he was being in the most awful of situations. It was hard to believe that the authorities in Britain could know what was going on and be doing nothing about it.

Johnny's morale was very low and it was an emotional experience listening to him describing to someone else how hard life was in a Moroccan jail. It seemed surreal that his voice could be being broadcast on television in England, but we couldn't get the authorities in Morocco who were dealing with the case to listen to what he had to say.

Hugh would later go to Morocco to make a documentary for ITN, having to talk his way out of being arrested two minutes after he started filming in Rabat.

Now that Jason was making a noise in London, the British Foreign Office had finally complained about Johnny being put in one of the worst jails in the country, and two weeks after his arrival he was moved to another jail in Rabat, called Salé. This meant that he was closer to the British Embassy and they could get in to see him more often than they had in Kenitra. John had been telling me the things he needed and I had arranged for money to be sent down to buy him supplies. I was liaising all the time over the phone and by email with the British Embassy, but nothing ever seemed to happen when we wanted it to. It was so frustrating to be so far away and so powerless to help. In one call John was desperate for toilet roll, not wanting to succumb to using his hand like the others, and that became my mission of the day.

The moment he left Kenitra he lost his access to the mobile phone and we were cut off from one another once more, with no idea how long it would be before we could speak again. Every time my phone rang my heart would skip a beat, but every time I was disappointed when I heard someone else's voice and not Johnny's.

John

I knew it was unusual for a prisoner to be moved in Morocco and I had no idea why I was being taken out of Kenitra after being there just a couple of weeks; no one ever explains anything to prisoners, particularly if there is a language barrier.

When I first arrived at Salé the authorities there obviously didn't have any idea who I was or why I had been sent to them, and they put me into solitary confinement while they worked out what to do with me. They assumed I was a terrorist. For a few hours the peace and quiet of being in a room alone was a relief, all the noise locked out by the door. After a few hours, however, I began to wonder how long I was going to be left there with absolutely nothing but the clothes on my back, all my belongings having been taken. Would I be able to cope with this silence for six months? The hours kept ticking past and I tried to ask the guards when they brought me food what was going on but their reply was always the same.

'No French. No English.'

The light stayed on all night and I was unable to sleep as my thoughts crowded in on me, no longer distracted and drowned out by the noises of a busy cell. I couldn't believe I was actually missing that rat-infested hole in Kenitra, but at least there I'd had some friends and access to a mobile phone.

I was discovering that no matter how low you got in life, there was always another layer beneath that one. The following day Anne-Marie from the embassy visited me and explained that they had insisted, after Jason got onto them, that I was taken out of Kenitra, which wasn't suitable for foreign prisoners. After three days I was moved out of solitary to a holding wing.

Salé was cleaner than Kenitra, and more European in style with bunk beds (although there weren't enough and I was still on the floor, being the new boy), but that brought with it the violence and the bullying I had experienced in Spain. The other problem was they had blockers so no one could use mobile phones. Suddenly Jane and I had been cut off from one another again, which made me feel completely desolate.

As I walked into my new cell, twenty-six new pairs of eyes turned to stare at me. I stood still, wondering what I should do. I remembered that I was meant to wait for the boss of the cell to greet me, but I didn't know which one he was. No one came forward to kiss me or welcome me. After a few awkward moments I made my way to the only space on the floor. I felt my bags being taken from my hands and tossed under a bunk. I could really have done with a cigarette, but it was Ramadan and there would be no smoking for several hours yet. Not being a Muslim I could have just lit up anyway, but I knew that wouldn't make me any friends and I badly needed some in this new, unknown environment.

No one spoke to me as I sat down cross-legged in the space in the centre of the cell. All their tongues were wagging, although no one was talking to me, just staring as they no doubt speculated about how I came to be there. I tried to count up the number of different cells I had been in over the previous year; I lost count after twenty-five. I kept telling myself that however bad this experience was, it had to be better than being in solitary, although if my latest cell-mates decided to take a dislike to me I might well wish I was alone again.

I tried to break the barrier and introduce myself to a few of the men sitting nearest to me, but they just shrugged my attempts at friendliness off. This was a very different welcome from the one I'd had in Kenitra. I was going to have to work hard here to win their respect. I obviously didn't hold the same novelty value in a big city jail, where they must have come across Europeans before.

EXTRADITED!

I spent hours of the first day with my gaze fixed on the television, avoiding their eyes, staring at pictures of life outside without understanding a word of what was being said. If ever my eyes strayed onto someone they would glare back at me and I would quickly revert to the screen.

Finally a man called Bashid, who spoke a little English, started to talk to me. It was a huge relief to find that I wasn't going to be ostracised forever. For the fol lowing few days I stuck to him like glue while I tried to work out the ways of the prison and how it was run. I needed to learn the rules fast to ensure I didn't tread on anyone's toes by sitting in the wrong place or using the toilet at the wrong time, or do anything without first checking it was okay.

Despite the fact that there were some bunks, the sleeping arrangements for those of us on the floor were the same as Kenitra, with us all lying on the hard con- crete in rows. The metal tubes of the bunks' structures were concreted into the ground, and cockroaches made their homes safely inside the tubes, pouring out onto the floor as soon as the daylight started to fade.

I had folded my blanket as many times as I could in the hope of deadening the pain a little, but it didn't work. I would sleep on my side for a while, and then turn onto my front. I would try sleeping on my hands, until they went numb. It was impossible to find a posi- tion that offered even a shred of comfort. People who had been there a long time had accumulated more blankets to cushion the hardness of the floor. They seemed to have got used to the discomfort and were able to sleep quite naturally. Journeys to the toilet or tap always seemed to bring grumbles and evil looks from those I couldn't avoid disturbing.

The problem with living at floor level was you never knew what you were going to put your hand on next. Often I would feel something slimy beneath my palms and realise it was a gob of someone's spittle. During the day, when other men went out of the cell to walk around and socialise, it was permissible for me to sit on their bunks, to stretch my muscles a bit. As soon as they came back, however, I would be brushed aside again, like a dog that has sneaked onto an armchair while his master was out of the room.

Whenever someone came back to the cell there always seemed to be a big story to recount, which would hold the rest of the cell in thrall, although I wouldn't have a clue what all the drama was about. I guess prison gossip was the only thing they had to keep their brains stimulated, apart from the constant warbling of the television.

There were some small slits high up in the wall to allow fresh air in, and it was just possible to peer out if I stood on tiptoe on the top bunk. All I could see was a brick wall and the sky, but at least it was daylight, something never visible to us in Kenitra. Even that tiny slice of a view made a change from staring at the television or the floor. The smells from the toilet weren't as suffocating on the top bunks, but the smoke was worse. It rose up towards the windows like a smog. For some reason, having to breathe other people's second-hand smoke is never the same as breathing your own.

As the days passed, two or three more of my fellow inmates started to communicate with me. I couldn't understand a word they said, and just kept nodding or shaking my head at what I hoped were appropriate points in their monologues, smiling and saying, 'si, si, si'. It was hard trying to look interested all the time, when actually all I wanted to do was crawl into a corner and cry.

A man started talking to me one day, asking if I was English.

'Yeah,' I replied, cautiously.

'Ah, Agadir,' he said cheerily. 'Agadir, '97. Drugs, big problem.'

'Yeah,' still wary.

'Me, me,' he pointed cheerfully at himself and I started to assume he must have been one of the drug smugglers. In the end it turned out that he was one of the policemen who had come on board to search the *Cygnet* when we docked in Agadir in 1997. I don't know how he recognised me after so long because I certainly didn't recognise him. Apparently he was inside for being bent and in the following days he told me stories about how many important people and top officials had ended up in prison because of the drugs bust. It seemed as if it had been the biggest story in the country at the time.

I had managed to make arrangements to have some more groceries brought in to me in Kenitra, but I was moved to Salé before they arrived, and so once more I was having to live on the generosity of others. Anne-Marie from the embassy would do her best to get supplies to me, but it would always take days to arrange anything. My new cell-mates seemed to be better off than the Kenitra ones. In Salé they often had more than one choice to offer round at a meal, with salads and bowls of olives and nuts to provide some variety to their diet.

Anne-Marie came in to see me when she could, but she was a very busy woman and there was a limit to how much time she could spend getting me things like a toilet roll, a bar of soap, a tube of toothpaste or a blanket. I never had a pillow and would roll up my trusty jacket and use that instead, so I was grateful when she brought me a good thick, heavy cushion, even though it gave me a cauliflower ear when I tried to lie on it for more than a few hours at a time. On one visit she assured me that once I was sentenced, things would become a lot easier because I would be moved on from the remand prison and they would be able to do things to help me.

Once I was sentenced? Her words hit me like a slap in the face. Did she think I was guilty, then? Did everyone at the British Embassy think that? Was that why they hadn't been making more of an effort to get me home? If they didn't think I was guilty, were they really just going to stand by and allow me to be sentenced? I left that visit feeling shell-shocked, trying to work out what I was actually feeling.

I wasn't allowed to write or receive letters, so I was back to trying to get phone calls through to Jane whenever I could persuade an inmate to rent me a mobile, which wasn't often and was never predictable. Jane would never know what time the calls would be coming, so sometimes she would be out. I eventually managed to bribe another prisoner to lend me his mobile phone (a packet of cigarettes in exchange for two minutes), but I couldn't get a signal because of the blockers so I had given up precious cigarettes for nothing. The same thing happened to me several times.

Despite the heat I managed to catch a head cold, which made my throat sore, my head ache and blocked my nose. The noise all around seemed to be growing all the time, battering against my brain twenty-four hours a day. I wasn't sure how much longer I could hold onto my sanity.

Jason wasn't able to get to see me in Salé, a serious city prison. In Kenitra he just had to turn up with a bag of sweets and a box of cigars and he was in. In Salé they informed him they would need official letters of permission in triplicate before they would let him near the place.

For my first hearing I was moved back to Kenitra, although it wasn't until we arrived and I was being processed yet again that the guards realised they had delivered me to the wrong jail, assuming I was going to Kenitra Central instead of Kenitra Civil. There were some loud and angry phone calls before they all worked out where I was meant to be and threw me back into the van. It was like I wasn't a person at all, just an inconvenient package that they all had a responsibility to look after for a while.

When I finally got to the right place, and back to the same cell I had been taken from originally, I was welcomed like a long-lost friend.

'Hey, Mr John!' they shouted, coming forward to shake my hand. I was relieved to see Said was still there and that night I was able to get back on the phone to Jane. Said showed me the most incredible generosity. The next time I was moved back to Salé he took the sim card out of his phone and gave it to me. In prison a sim card is like gold dust, but he didn't hesitate. It meant that I could borrow people's phones without having to ask them for credit, which made it much easier to approach someone and ask to use their phone.

I kept it hidden in a hole in the Velcro strap of my sandals, where it had come slightly apart. Even when the guards took my shoes off to search them, they didn't think to look inside the lining of the strap, and the card was small enough for them not to be able to feel it through the material. Every time I was searched my heart would be in my mouth, always aware that if I angered them or was seen to break the rules I could end up being beaten or taken off to solitary confinement again.

The telephone blockers in Salé meant we never got to talk for more than thirty seconds or a minute at a time before the signal was cut, and poor Jane would spend hours dialling and re-dialling, trying to get a new connection. Having hardly any credit on the card I had to do the 'three rings' trick and sometimes Freya would pick up by mistake on the first or second ring and I would immediately lose a few precious pennies of credit. I tried to organise a similar arrangement with Mum, but because the calls were so infrequent she would forget and pick up as well. Everything was so hard.

Just moving from Kenitra to Salé cost me seven packs of cigarettes by way of payment to every guard I came into contact with. They only cost a few pence a packet, but it was still a drain on my limited and dwindling resources.

A year after I was arrested in Spain, and around a month after arriving in Morocco, the day of my hearing arrived. In the few phone calls I had managed to get through to England, Jane and Catherine had told me that Jason believed I would be released that day.

I was excited at the prospect of finally being free, determined to stay positive despite all the previous disappointments, while at the same time bracing myself for yet another fall. It was a difficult mental tightrope to walk. In a few days' time I would either be ecstatically happy, back home on the island with Jane and my family, or I would be totally devastated, looking at two more months or more awaiting a trial, and maybe twenty or thirty more years of sentence to serve if I was found guilty. I realised that if they decided to send me for trial the chances were I would be found guilty. I had heard that in Morocco acquittal for drug-related offences was unheard of.

I kept hearing terrible stories about long sentences being handed out to innocent people. Regardless of that, I was willing to believe that Jason was right and that he would be taking me home to England with him that evening after the hearing, but what if he was wrong? What if I was just another innocent man who was going to be wrongly imprisoned?

Jason wasn't allowed into the courtroom and I sat next to Ben, who seemed unduly meek and cowed in front of the judge. I wished Jason could be there, demanding to be listened to, treating the judge as an equal rather than some deity. Jane and Catherine had sent down some smarter clothes for me with Jason, but I was still in the same scruffy shoes that had been with me all year. I hadn't looked in a mirror for weeks, so I dread to think what my hair and beard looked like. The weeks of just sitting on the floor had given me a hunched posture and an arched back, which was hard to straighten. My knees were also painful, as if I had been sitting in a cramped aeroplane for several days, forcing me to move slowly. I must have looked like a broken man.

The courtroom settled down and the case began, most of it floating past me in a sea of unintelligible words. Ben had a huge file of papers in front of him, which had been carefully prepared for him by Jane, Catherine and Jason, and he had been briefed over and over again on what he had to say, what points he had to make. But as everyone else kept talking, he remained silent, writing notes with his head down. Every time I nudged him to say something in my defence he would hush me, and tell me this wasn't the right moment.

'Show them the documents,' I would plead.

'That comes later,' he kept assuring me.

Ben's advice to me had always been that I shouldn't worry, that we all have little hiccups in our lives. Personally, I thought the prospect of spending the rest of my life in Moroccan jail was more than a little hiccup and wished he would approach the whole case with a little more urgency.

The judge had a list of questions, which he asked me through an interpreter. I gave my answers in English, the interpreter put them back into Arabic and the judge would then tell the court scribe what to write down. The scribe then read his words back to the interpreter, who put them into English for me and, at the end of each page, I was asked to sign that they were the words I had said. It took three and a half hours to ask me about five questions.

At the end of the three and a half hours I assumed there would be a recess and then Ben would get his chance to put my case later in the day, but later never happened. At the end of the question-and-answer session I was taken back to a holding cell. Jason, Ben and Anne-Marie came down to see me. They told me that was the end of the hearing. The judge had found out all he wanted to know and would now make his decision as to whether I should go to trial. It seemed he wasn't going to get to hear any of the arguments we had carefully put together. When Ben had said he would be putting the points 'later', he meant at the trial. It seemed he, like Anne-Marie, thought I was on my way to a conviction.

'We haven't got a result yet,' Jason admitted. 'We will have to wait a few days before we find out what the judge is going to do.'

I could see that he was as shocked by the way things had turned out as I was. He had been so confident he would be taking me home with him that evening he had even booked my ticket. The judge, it seemed, didn't want to take responsibility for setting me free, just in case it turned out he had made a mistake.

Once the hearing was over they put me back into a van to return from Kenitra to Salé. Instead of climbing onto a plane with Jason and heading back to Jane and the rest of my family, I was heading back to a jail full of hostile strangers.

Walking back in my cell in Salé after expecting to be freed was painful. Jason had been so certain I would be going home with him that I had finally dared to let myself hope he was right. Now I had to readjust my mind and go back to the waiting and hoping game. Jason was still positive, promising that it would be a matter of days before he managed to sort things out, but I was beginning to think he knew no more than the rest of us. It was all right for him to be upbeat and positive, he was probably already sitting back at the Hilton Hotel with a cool drink.

I stared at the television in the corner of the cell, which was showing the same soap opera it showed every day, and wondered if this would be the last time I would have to sit through it. I'd wondered the same thing a couple of days before, and here I was again. When the food came round I wondered if it would be the last time I would have to eat a prison meal or wash with a bucket of cold water. As I lay down on the floor to try to snatch some sleep I wondered if this was the last time I would have to do without my own bed, or the last time I had to wake up to find cockroaches tangled in my hair. It was like standing on the edge of a precipice. If I allowed myself to think about the possibility that I might be in cells like this one for the next twenty or so years,

I would be in danger of plunging off the edge into a bottomless pit of despair. I had to have these slender hopes to cling on to.

I had grown sloppy about bothering to wash, telling myself I would save it for my first hot shower at whatever hotel I was taken to on release. I even found myself looking at the sell-by date on a carton of yoghurt, thinking I would be home before the time it had to be eaten.

Jason had still been so confident he had told me he wasn't going to fly out till the following day because he knew I would be going with him, giving the impression he was sure the judge would make the right decision. I knew for a fact, because Anne-Marie had told me, there weren't any flights that day anyway so he had no choice but to stay on for another day, but it was nice of him to at least pretend that he was putting himself out for me. Anne-Marie was equally optimistic in her pronouncements, assuring me I would be on my way home any day now. It seemed that at least we had managed to convince her that I was innocent, if not the judge.

I had managed to get my Walkman back and had a tape of the comedian Roy Chubby Brown. I felt so uplifted, despite all my fears, that for the first time in over a year I found myself actually laughing. But at the same time, my head was constantly aching. I had never felt so anxious before. If this decision went against me and they decided to send me to trial I was pretty sure

I would end up with a long sentence. No one in authority would want to lose face by admitting they had made a mistake by that stage. If I didn't walk free within the next day or two I was afraid I might finally crack under the strain.

CHAPTER SEVEN

Jane

It was two weeks after the hearing that Jason called to tell me that the judge had decided Johnny should go to trial. Everything we had tried to do to get the truth across to them had failed. It seemed no one in the Moroccan judicial system had taken the trouble to read all the material we had put together for them, any more than they had in Spain. I could tell Jason was shocked. He felt he had been left with egg on his face after being so confident and raising our hopes so high. It sounded to me like he was taking this failure personally. He seemed to be intending to keep up the fight, which was encouraging.

I'd had the press camping out of the doorstep, waiting to hear the answer, all of them as sure as we had been that Johnny would be home soon, and all of them keen to be the first to get the story.

The frightening thing was that if the Moroccan government decided they would put Johnny on trial, it was very unlikely they would want to climb down and admit they had made a mistake. They were going to be doing their utmost to get a conviction, and we had seen how easily they could get their way when they were determined. The hearing had been their last chance to sweep the whole case aside; now there would be even more reputations resting on them getting a conviction. It looked as if all Johnny's worst predictions were coming true. How could I argue with him now when he said he could end up being locked up for the next twenty or thirty years? I had tried everything I could think of. If a lawyer like Jason couldn't save Johnny, who could?

I was going to have to pass the news on to Johnny when I next managed to get through to him on the phone. It would be the bleakest phone call I would ever have to make to him. I had no reassurances to offer him, no new initiatives in the pipeline that I could talk about – nothing.

Jason had had to come back to England because his wife was having a baby, but he was still determined to fight on. His next weapon was going to be to get support from as many celebrities as he could, raising Johnny's profile. He intended to make as big a noise as possible. At that moment it seemed like rather a futile gesture. If the Moroccans wouldn't listen to reasoned arguments from lawyers and politicians, what hope was there that they would respond to a bunch of actors, singers and writers?

The most frustrating thing was that we weren't allowed to have an English lawyer representing Johnny in court during the trial; we were going to have to rely on Ben, which didn't seem promising on the evidence so far. Jason wanted to make a fuss and asked Andrew Turner to raise the question with Tony Blair in the House of Commons.

Andrew stood up in Parliament and asked Tony Blair why a British lawyer representing a British citizen detained in a Moroccan prison, such as John Packwood, was not allowed access to the courtroom or prison to see his client. The Prime Minister answered that he knew nothing about the case. We knew this wasn't true because of all the signed replies that had come back to people who had written to him on Johnny's behalf, and he later had to write and apologise to Andrew for giving him an erroneous answer as he had been briefed incorrectly. It was nice of him to write and admit he was wrong, but no help to us.

The British Ambassador in Morocco, who Jason had been to see with the full dossier of information on the case, was also now taking a personal interest, having been alerted to just how grave a miscarriage of justice was about to happen. But it was all beginning to look like too little too late. I feared that Johnny wouldn't be able to cope with such a barrage of disappointments.

John

After two weeks' agonising wait, Jane told me the judge had decided I should stand trial. All the hopes that I had been building up, encouraged by Jason and Anne-Marie's optimism, were shattered in a moment as I listened to her voice on a mobile in the corner of the cell, trying to make sense of her words above the noise, while expecting to be cut off by the blockers at any moment. We had wasted a whole year trying to avoid something that had proved to be inevitable. I could have come straight to Morocco when I was arrested and we would have been in the same position. All the work Jane and Catherine had put in had come to nothing; all the money we had spent on lawyers had been wasted. No one was taking any notice of anything we had to say. The people who had the power to take away the rest of my life believed I was guilty.

The thoughts went round and round in my head; maybe if we had done this, or maybe if we hadn't done that, things would have turned out differently. But in fact I knew we had tried everything we possibly could. Jane and Catherine and their loyal band of helpers had lobbied everyone they could, written to everyone they could, even been blackmailed. They had given a year of their lives to trying to avoid me being extradited and going to trial, and it was as if it was all in vain. The system was just grinding on and now it looked as if it would crush my life once and for all.

There was nothing I could do to distract myself from my doomed thoughts. I couldn't even listen to my favourite music on my Walkman because it would remind me of happy times that I might now never recapture. It was as if I was hypnotised with my own misery, unable to tear myself away from my own mind. I didn't want to play the tapes that Jane had scooped from the car and sent down to me in Spain, partly because I was worried that if I listened to them in prison they would forever remind me of these terrible times and I would never be able to get pleasure from listening to them again. I knew from previous experiences over the last year that when my spirits were plunged that low it would take at least a week before I would be able to lift them back to anything like a bearable level. To be trapped in a cell with people you can't communicate with for twenty-four hours a day, when you are at your lowest, is an experience I would never have believed I could survive.

The authorities told us the trial would start in five weeks, which took us to the period between Christmas and the New Year, when everyone in England, including Jason, would be on their winter holidays. They refused to give us a definite date until the end of Ramadan. As usual, nothing was certain, nothing was predictable. There seemed to be no reality I could get a grasp on. All hope was gone. I now thought the most likely outcome would be that they would sentence me to ten years, which seemed to be the standard sort of sentence for drug offenders. I had talked to a number of foreigners in the various jails I had been in and most of the ones who knew nothing about the crimes they were accused of seemed to get ten years.

I was now becoming convinced I would never see my mother alive again, and it was more than I could hope that Jane would wait ten years for me. Her support over the previous year had been incredible, but she had a daughter and a life to live – she couldn't be expected to dedicate everything to me if I was going to be gone that long.

Having watched Ben in action in the courtroom for the hearing, I didn't think he was the man for the job of defending me during the trial. We were going to have to find someone else, but it would need to be someone who was also willing to smuggle me in the odd bit of money, as Ben had been doing, because I was going to need to pay for a lot of things, not least phone calls and bribes. Without money I would be reduced to the helpless state of the boys I had seen hanging from the bars in Kenitra: beaten and abused.

I had heard that there was a big celebration coming up for the fiftieth anniversary of the country's independence, and that the king of Morocco was going to be pardoning thousands of prisoners as a result, but I didn't hold out any hope that I would be included, since I hadn't even been tried or sentenced yet. My alleged offence was also to do with drugs, which was another reason I would not be eligible for a King's pardon.

King Mohammed VI has been on the throne since 1999. His family have ruled since the seventeenth century and are believed to be descended from the Prophet Mohammed. Criticism of the monarchy is absolutely forbidden and the king is both a monarch and a spiritual leader, or 'Commander of the Faithful', as they prefer to put it. Although trade unions, political parties and professional bodies can take an active part in public life, the king still holds ultimate power. If we couldn't even get judges to listen to our pleas, what hope would we have of reaching a man as exulted as him?

Now that the staff at the British Embassy had become convinced of my innocence, they were keen to show they were doing whatever they could to look after me. When I was moved back to Kenitra again and into my old cell in preparation for the trial, Anne-Marie saw the sores on my legs when she visited and insisted on speaking to the director about having me moved to a less flea-ridden cell, as if there was such a thing anywhere in Morocco. The director obliged her by putting me into a smaller, nine-man cell, which was not nearly as friendly as the other cells I'd been in. The inmates had settled themselves in for the long-haul life sentences they had been given and had set up a lucrative drugs business.

The worst thing was that in the confusion of the move from one cell to another, I wasn't able to get my sim card out of Said's phone, so I was cut off from Jane once more. I immediately started plotting how to get back to the other wing to retrieve it.

The cell was small, but it had a window and concrete bunks so at least I was raised off the floor. As soon as I'd settled in I gave all my clothes a wash and stuck them out the window to dry, one by one. Washing stopped me thinking and helped to keep me sane. It was quieter than the other cells; the inmates didn't have the television blaring all day long and they didn't seem to pray for so long at night. From the window it was possible to see the roofs and minarets of Kenitra and even a bridge and some people in the distance. Every few hours they would switch on the loudspeakers to call the faithful to prayer, particularly during Ramadan. It was like they were all competing to see who could be the loudest, battling for business. I could remember when I was in Saudi the Imams used to do the chanting themselves and the sound was quite romantic, but in Kenitra it sounded like they were using the tinniest of cheap recordings.

Despite the mosques it was still better than the other cells. Being in a different part of the prison we couldn't hear the dogs barking and I was able to get a good night's sleep for the first time for a long time, only waking up when I grew cold because I was using my only blanket as a mattress to soften the hard concrete of the bunk.

Although Kenitra was sweltering during the day it could be freezing at night. When I got some of my clothes back from Salé I used them as extra padding between my hips and the concrete bunk, and some as draught-proofing round the window. One night I even managed to sleep for twelve hours, with only a few returns to consciousness along the way. It was my first lie-in for over a year.

When the television was switched on I was forced to watch some of the programmes that I thought I would miss when I had seen the trailers in Salé. I no longer allowed myself to hope I would soon be out. I knew I had to start to come to terms with the possibility of a long sentence. If things went wrong I didn't want it to be a shock or a disappointment when the sentencing was announced, I wanted to get my mind into a place where it would be able to accept the worst possible news without cracking up on me.

The only sounds in the cell at night came from the railway line outside, but I found the chugging of the engines and the clicking of the tracks quite soothing compared with all the noises I'd had to grow used to over the previous year. The sound of trains reminded me of my Auntie Molly's house in Leamington Spa, where I used to visit as a child, and of old American movies set in New York.

On my first night there someone stole the boss's phone charger, sending him into a boiling rage. He even kicked over the cooking pot, splashing the contents of what was to be that day's meal all over the floor as he ranted and raved.

The boss was called Abdul Ghada. He was a fat, unpleasant man who sat around issuing orders and accepting gifts like a sultan and ran the prison's main drug business with a liquidiser. He and his helpers had a highly profitable system set up. They would take one packet of high quality hash, and three packets of low quality. They would then churn the whole mixture into a fine powder in the liquidiser and spoon it into the plastic wrappers that came off packets of tea. They would then Sellotape the packets shut and lay them under their blankets for the night, pressing them tight with the weight of their bodies. Finally they would take a hot knife to smooth the packets over, which would melt the powder into a solid lump, making it look firmer and darker, disguising the fact that it was just a pale powder inside.

The next day the product would be for sale on the wing. I watched their operation in a mixture of amazement and awe. Lumps of their raw material were hidden in home-made boxes constructed of cardboard that was thick enough to be able to make holes in the side, slide the drugs in and insert a cardboard block on top to hide it. They would finally sew plastic over the edges of the boxes to hide their handiwork. Each day the boss would undo the stitches in the boxes, pull out the wedges and open up his hidey-holes. He kept his phone in a similar place. Everyone in the prison was making these boxes. I would see them in transit all over the prison, knowing that at least half of them had secret compartments for smuggling.

For an hour each day the cell doors would be opened for exercise and the place would become a hive of activity as people came to buy their drugs, just as we used to go to the prison shop in Valdemoro for food and drink. Most of the customers were young boys, trading precious food that their parents had brought in to them. I felt sorry for the poor families who thought they were providing nourishment and treats for their children like dates and coffee, only to have it swapped for a few puffs of this low-grade hash. Even the guards would take some of his product from time to time, no doubt in exchange for turning a blind eye to the liquidiser. I remembered the prison director asking, 'Do you smoke hashish?' before putting me in the cell, which made me wonder if the authorities knew all about it and allowed it to continue because it helped to keep things calm and quiet.

Everyone was poor in Kenitra, even the ones who had the most. Every time I opened my bag I was aware of at least five pairs of eyes straining to look inside to see what I might have that they could ask for. The trouble with living out of a bag was that every time I needed something, such as a T-shirt, I had to carefully unpack and pack again in front of everyone. I learnt to open and close the zip as sneakily as possible, but someone would always see something, whether it was a razor, socks, towel or jumper, and would ask if they could have it later in the day. In every cell I had been in, I always seemed to be the only one who ever had a cigarette lighter.

'John, John, *brica!*' was a phrase I would hear all day long as everyone lit up around me, trying to save their own gas. Other phrases I heard constantly were, 'English, do you have … ?' or 'Give me, give me …'

Abdul Ghada kept things like chocolate in his own private treasure chest. Stored in a cardboard box he would bring things out to gloat over once he thought the rest of us were asleep – like Fagin in *Oliver Twist*. No one ever protested because he was the boss and the respect for bosses was absolute. His favourite phrase to me was, 'Tony Blair, George Bush, no good!' I didn't necessarily disagree with him, but the constant repetition became tedious.

'Bin Laden no good,' I would occasionally reply when I was feeling belligerent, taking the sting out of my impudence with what I hoped was a conciliatory shrug, as if we were both in agreement that all warmon-gering leaders were the same.

'England, America, no good!' he would insist, deter-mined to let me know that I was an outsider in his world and must behave as such.

He seemed to be very good at telling me what I couldn't do, which was virtually anything I actually start-ed to do, but he would never actually guide me as to what I could do. If I went to wash he would tell me I couldn't. If I went to the toilet he would shake his head and wave me back to my seat. If I wanted to make a drink he would tell me to wait. It was increasingly obvi-ous he didn't like me, but I took consolation from the fact that I wasn't the only one he picked on. He seemed to enjoy being nasty to everyone, doing things like turn-ing the television off when they were watching, or turning the screen so that only he could see it.

I always did as he asked because I knew if I gave him any cause for complaint I would be moved to another cell and would have to start all over again ingratiating myself with a new set of people.

Just before he left Morocco, Jason promised me he wouldn't be giving up the struggle, that he would bring on board all his celebrity friends like George Clooney, Hugh Grant, Annie Lennox, Mariella Frostrup (who was also his wife), Phil Manzanera from Roxy Music, the film director Richard Curtis, the theatre director and writer Nick Kent and actors Gina Bellman, Keely Hawes, Maryam d'Abo, Joseph Fiennes and Matthew Mcfadden. Outside show business, there was the artist Damien Hirst and the author Nick Hornby, Andrew Turner MP, Sam Bourne of the Yacht Harbour Association, the art dealer Jay Jopling, the author and economist Noreena Hertz, Rodney Carr of the Royal Yachting Association, David Green of the UK Sailing Academy, John Clarke of the British Marine Federation, Roger Alton, the editor of the *Observer* and the documentary-maker Nick Broomfield.

Mark Knopfler of Dire Straits had already heard of my case and expressed an interest in helping when he met Jason, who assured me big names like that would help to draw people's attention to my desperate situation. After hearing that Mark Knopfler was interested in helping I seemed to hear his songs coming from other people's cells all the time, singing about washing machines and televisions. I was glad Jason was still so keen to keep fighting, but I didn't hold out much hope of success. It was beginning to worry me that the Moroccans actually did think I was guilty as charged, regardless of all the evidence we were putting forward in my defence, and, if they thought that, they weren't likely to let me go just because a few celebrities put their names to a petition.

Some of the celebrities were willing to take action themselves. Annie Lennox suggested writing a song about my plight and Damien Hirst offered to sell a painting to raise funds for the cause. George Clooney, who had recently been to Morocco to film *Syriana*, agreed to write a personal letter to the king. He told the king how much he had enjoyed being in his beautiful country and hoped that he would be able to come back and film again. He then respectfully mentioned that he was taking an interest in my case because he was a personal friend of Jason, my lawyer. He asked if the king would be kind enough to consider granting me a pardon, and ended with an open invitation to his majesty to attend the premier of *Syriana* in Los Angeles, or any other country he chose, as his honoured guest. That someone as busy as George Clooney would be willing to take the time and trouble to plead my case so diplomatically touched me. He might not have turned up on the tarmac of the airport to rescue me with Brad Pitt, as I had fantasised, but he had done the next best thing. It didn't seem likely, however, that a letter from an actor, even one as distinguished as him, would sway a king.

On 11 November 2005, I was moved back to Salé, without any explanation, and put into the same cell as before. Just as I had managed to acquire five blankets for my bunk in Kenitra, I was back with one blanket on the floor of the same cell I had been in before. Whenever I took a step forward, I always seemed to be made to take two steps back.

As I arrived in the guardhouse the screws were tucking into a lavish meal cooked by the inmates. It was an amazing banquet. I mentioned it to a German who spoke a little English (one of only two Europeans in the prison apart from me).

'It happens every day,' he told me.

'If I was a prison guard I don't think I would ever risk taking food off the men who hated them so much,' I muttered.

It seemed extraordinary to me that the prisoners would be willing to hand over what looked like their best food to people who beat and tortured them, took their food and cigarettes, and that the guards trusted them not to spit in it, or worse.

There were two electric cooking rings in our cell, but there still always seemed to be somebody hassling me when I was waiting for the water to boil for a coffee. Sometimes it would reach the boil and someone would help themselves to it before I had a chance and I would have to start all over again with cold water. I was sick of drinking lukewarm coffee.

The king was appearing on television. He often appeared, being filmed shaking hands with dignitaries and kissing the masses, but this time I was more interested in what was happening than usual. He was announcing who was going to be pardoned to celebrate the fiftieth anniversary of Morocco's independence.

There were 12,000 Moroccans pardoned and 300

foreigners. I knew Jason had submitted a request for me to be one of them, but I held out no hope; I hadn't even been tried yet and in order to obtain a pardon the paperwork needed to have been submitted months before. Maybe in another ten years it would be possible. However, despite all the disappointments I had suffered in the past, I couldn't help feeling encouraged. The odds were against it, but this man, who I was forever seeing on the television, held a key to my freedom.

The announcement came; if you had one year left to serve of a ten-year sentence, or six months of a five-year sentence, you would be allowed out. When the announcement was made on the television all the men who knew they fell into that category were shouting and cheering and jubilantly throwing things around the cells. The noise emitting from around 800 men was deafening. They all believed it was Allah answering the thousands of prayers they had offered up since being locked up. I had no hopes that Allah would look kindly on anything I might ask of him.

The following morning I was woken by a kick in the ribs from one of the guards.

'Hurry, hurry, hurry,' he ordered impatiently. 'Pack up stuff!'

Assuming I was being moved yet again I rushed to pack all my belongings before I was dragged out, always nervous about leaving something precious behind during these sudden moves. I was led out into the main courtyard of the prison where hundreds of other prisoners were filing in from every direction, standing in lines in the centre with their bags in front of them. I couldn't work out what was going on. Guards started walking down the lines, opening up all the bags, turfing the contents out onto the ground, searching for God knows what. I assumed I was on my way to yet another prison, but why were there so many of us? And why were the others smiling and patting one another on the back? They seemed a bit happy for a bunch of prisoners. I wondered if it could have something to do with the pardons being issued, but I didn't even dare think about it, knowing how terrible the disappointment could be if I allowed myself to get my expectations up.

One by one they handcuffed us and herded us into waiting vans. Once the vans were filled to bursting they drove us to the police station and unloaded us again. Our handcuffs were then removed and we were ordered to line up once more. They took each of our names and the men in front of me were called into an office, one at a time. After a couple of minutes they would come out again. I saw a man who had been in the same van as me go in; when he came out I noticed he had what looked like his passport in his hand. For the first time I allowed myself a glimmer of hope. Maybe this could be it; maybe I actually was going to be going home. But then I thought it was more likely, as I had been given my trial date, to be the long-awaited three-day questioning that I had been warned would happen.

I saw Anne-Marie from the embassy coming up the stairs. I looked at her, feeling increasingly confused.

'It's over. Don't worry, John,' she smiled, 'it's over. You've been pardoned.'

I went across the room and threw my arms around her, hugging her tightly, tears welling up in my eyes. I felt my knees wobbling and knew I was in danger of collapsing from a mixture of shock and relief. She came into the little office with me and the police asked what my intentions were.

'Mr Packwood will be leaving the country today,' Anne Marie piped up.

The policeman nodded his approval of this plan and passed over my passport. I walked out of the station in a dream, hardly able to believe that I was actually free, expecting to be called back any second. Anne-Marie led me to a waiting car, which sped us away to the embassy.

'Am I really going home today?' I asked.

'Well, actually your flight's tomorrow morning, but it is the first flight out.'

We drove on with me in a daze.

'Hello, John, old chap,' the British Ambassador greeted me as I was ushered into his office. 'Fancy a cup of tea?'

It is hard to imagine the pleasure to be had from simple things like tea with fresh milk and a china cup, with some cake and biscuits on the side when you have been without

them for so long. There was a picture of the Queen looking down at us reassuringly as we sat on leather sofas and
chatted like it was just another normal day.

'Would you like to phone home?' the ambassador
asked.

'Oh, yes please.' It didn't seem possible that things
could suddenly be so easy when it had been such a struggle for so long. I called Jane, who had been told I was
going to be released but didn't know what was happening.

'I'm coming home tomorrow,' I told her, hardly able
to get the words out.

Jane

Jason had decided that he would apply for a King's pardon for Johnny at the same time as everything else he was planning, feeling he had nothing left to lose, that every avenue was worth exploring. It seemed like even more of an outside chance since our application only went in the day before the pardons were going to be announced. The ambassador in Morocco agreed to meet up personally with one of the king's representatives to plead John's case. It all seemed like too much of a rush job for there to be any chance of success. When John managed to call me that night it was one of the worst phone calls we had ever had. I had nothing positive to tell him and he held out no hope of the pardon being granted.

The next day my phone rang and it was Jason.

'He's out,' he said.

'What do you mean?' His words didn't seem to make any sense. How could Johnny be out?

'The king has pardoned him and he's been released. It seems George's letter has worked.'

After all those months of false hopes and dashed expectations, it had just happened as instantly and apparently as easy as that. Even though he had never been charged, never been questioned and never been tried, somehow he had been pardoned. All it took was a word from the king and all the problems and obstacles that had proved so impossible to overcome had just melted away. Lords, ladies, baronesses, MPs, MEPs, mayors, ambassadors, lawyers and the media had all tried for a year to exert their influence on our behalf and none of them had got anywhere, but one letter from a Hollywood film star and everything had changed. I tried to reassure myself that the £80,000 and the year we spent collecting all the evidence and facts of the case had also contributed. After all, it had all given Jason a crystal clear picture and the certainty that Johnny needed to come home.

I made Jason repeat exactly what the situation was twice, but I still couldn't really take it in. It wasn't until the embassy called fifteen minutes later and confirmed everything that I actually believed Johnny might finally be coming home. By the time I received John's call from the embassy, the news had reached the media, and they were inside my house as we talked.

The following day I was escorted by the media to Heathrow. The arrivals board threw us into a panic, announcing that the plane had landed early and we rushed to the lounge. As the group of friends and family grew we found ourselves surrounded by more and more cameras and reporters.

Clinging to Catherine, in a state of emotional meltdown, I watched each new wave of people coming through the doors, the tension building all the time as I searched for Johnny's face. A Reuters reporter was the first to tell us he had landed, that they had spoken to him and he was on his way. Johnny was coming home and I didn't know whether to laugh with happiness or cry with relief. Our relationship had been knocked off its axis a year earlier and I had been forced to take the reins, given the small bit of power we had over our destinies. Now it was swinging back and I realised it was going to be another huge adjustment to our lives. I wondered how well I was going to cope.

Over the previous year I had discovered an entirely different world from the one I had lived in all my life. I now knew all about South American drug cartels and how they worked, maximum security prisons and all the corruption involved, and international blackmailers and con-men. I knew about Interpol and political compromises. All the stuff that had always been safely contained in books and films and television programmes had impinged on my life. Now that I knew that all these people were out there, all around us, I would never be able to forget it. We had both had our eyes opened to the reality of the world we had been living in; our blissful ignorance had been shattered. In the end, Johnny had only been given his life back on the whim of one, powerful man. Things could easily have ended differently and there would have been nothing we could have done about it. We would never feel completely safe again, now that we knew safety was just an illusion and could be whipped away from us at any moment.

John

On Thursday 17 November, after leaving the embassy, I was sitting in a hotel room, running my first hot bath for over a year. I had changed worlds in just a few hours and had had my freedom restored as abruptly and unexpectedly as I had had it snatched away. I felt dazed at the speed with which everything had turned round.

The same rubbish soap opera I'd been watching for the previous two months was playing on the television. The people from the embassy had seemed to be amazed that I was out. Why were they so amazed? Had they thought I was guilty all along? Jason wasn't surprised, of course.

'I fucking told you I'd get you out,' were his first words when he came on the line from England. It was true; he had always said he would get me out, even at the moments when everything seemed to be failing.

The bath was so hot as I sank beneath the water, I thought I might be going to pass out or have a heart attack. 'Not now,' I begged silently as my heart thumped at full speed, 'not now I'm out, not after all that.' Gradually it slowed back to a normal pace and I relaxed into the warmth of the water. I was out of prison and I had a night in a hotel bed stretching in front of me. I started to scrub at the layer of grime that had been coating my skin for so long. To be alone and quiet and private was so wonderful I almost felt guilty. As my head swam gently from the mixture of relief, exhaustion and heat I allowed myself to imagine what it would feel like to fly home the next day and arrive in the cool, green island of my birth.

Once I was out of the bath and dressed again I decided to go outside for a walk, just because I could, because I was no longer a prisoner. I thought I would find a bar, have a few beers and then stagger back to my bed. I knew the embassy car would be coming for me at nine o'clock the next morning to take me to the airport and I had no other responsibilities beyond making sure I was ready for collection.

There was a lot of celebrating going on in the streets for the fiftieth anniversary of the country's independence; there was a carnival atmosphere. Every corner I came to there was a policeman or two, all with guns in their holsters, their eyes darting around, looking for trouble. I remembered the first time officials had just plucked me out of the passport queue in Spain and I was acutely aware of just how easily something like that can happen. I began to feel nervous. By the time I got to the end of the street I decided it was not a risk worth taking, and walked speedily back to the safety of the hotel lobby. There I had a few small bottles of lager, which went straight to my head, before going up to bed, singing and dancing happily to myself. It was the first decent night's sleep I had enjoyed in a year.

The next morning a chauffeur arrived dead on time, took my bags and loaded them into the boot of the car and drove me for a couple of hours to Casablanca. It felt so good to be cruising past the shanty towns by the sides of the roads, understanding better now how hard life was for the inhabitants, and also knowing that I was now on my way out of there.

When we got to the airport the driver insisted on taking my bags through and checking me in. I guess he had been instructed to make sure I got on that flight. He was probably watching me all the way out to the aeroplane steps, waiting for the door to shut behind me and the plane to take off.

I was sitting next to a nice couple, who were on their way back from holiday in Morocco. I told them my story. I'm not sure they believed me but they kept nodding their heads sympathetically. It was the first real, long conversation I'd had in English with anyone for a long time. My first sight of England was as we came over the Isle of Wight. I was overcome with indescribable feelings of anticipation, relief and euphoria. It really was over. All I wanted to do was parachute out and get home.

The moment we disembarked, the Reuters corre-
spondent who works airside at Heathrow was there
with questions, hoping to get his story before I talked
to all the other media waiting on the other side. Jane
and I had talked already about what we would do when
I was reunited with everyone; we had agreed that the
first person I should go up to must be Mum, as I hadn't
seen her at all for a year. I'd give her a kiss for the
cameras, and then I would go to Catherine and Jane,
then Jason and the others. I did it just as planned. It was
so good to see Mum and to give her a hug, after being
so fearful that I might never see her again. We were
then bundled into cars to be taken to a press conference
at a local hotel.

In the course of the short journey I was warned about
certain things it would be politically and diplomatically
unwise to talk about, given that there were other Britons
still trapped in Moroccan jails, hoping for pardons. I tried
to remember everything they told me but my head was
swimming with the suddenness of it all.

The next thing I knew we were in a hotel conference
room in front of a scrum of press. After trying so hard
and for so long to be invisible it was a shock to suddenly be the centre of attention and to have a clamour of
questions coming at me. Although I was elated to be
home, it was a big adjustment as well. Not having had
any decisions to make for myself for over a year, a part of
my brain had switched off, and it was disconcerting

coming back to the normal world. Someone asked how the experience had changed my life and what I thought lay ahead.

'A year of my life has been taken,' I said, 'but I can't do anything about getting that back.' The thoughts that I had been mulling over and over during the previous months started to formulate into words, my sadness at what I had lost beginning to turn into anger towards those who had taken so much from me. 'I've spent my life's savings'; I paused and smiled, not wanting to spoil such a magical moment with bitterness about something I could do nothing about; 'But at least my mother's alive, my dog needs a walk and my girl's not run off with the milkman.'

When the ferry finally deposited us safely back on the island later that day, it felt almost like I had never been away.

EPILOGUE

John

Luckily it was winter and Cowes was empty of tourists, so when I got home I was able to potter about my home town and get myself reoriented without too much interruption. In summer, when the harbour is buzzing with boats, the streets can be crowded and confusing. I would have found it hard getting myself back into the swing of a life of freedom without those winter months to adapt.

I couldn't decide what to do first. I wanted to do everything; drive round the island, go and see all my old friends, get to work on my boat or take Badger for a walk.

It's been a year now and I'm still finding it hard to motivate myself to start rebuilding my savings and getting my career going again. Although I am safely out of prison I still can't risk travelling abroad and I still haven't really had my name officially cleared, leaving me in something of a limbo.

I have recovered in most ways, but with recovery has come anger at what was done to me and for what is being done to many other prisoners around the world who are just as innocent of the crimes they are accused of as I was.

The really frightening thing about this story is that it could happen to anyone. One morning you could think you were setting out for a week's holiday, feeling good about the way your life is going, and by the end of the day you could find yourself imprisoned in a foreign country, unable to understand what is being said to you and with no idea why you are there or how you are going to get yourself freed. Savings that you have spent the last twenty years building up could then vanish as you struggle to clear your name and get home to continue your life, never knowing if you are going to be there for days, weeks, months or years.

But it isn't only the person who has been arrested who has their life turned upside down. As in bereavement, where relatives and friends are left struggling to come to terms with their loss, those whose everyday lives are entwined with the wrongly imprisoned are plunged into an equally nightmarish situation as they battle to free their loved ones, with no idea how long it will be before they see them again, or even if they ever will. The ripple effect goes far and wide, washing through families like a tidal wave.

Any individual who falls into the grip of the international diplomatic, political and legal systems is soon reminded of how helpless we all are in the face of uncaring, cruel bureaucracies. A person could die in a prison cell hundreds of miles from their home before the relevant authorities are able to understand that a mistake has been made and a terrible injustice performed.

In 2006, Henry, a fellow crew member on the boat to Agadir with me, went on holiday to Italy and was arrested in exactly the same way I was. Despite all the publicity my case had received, the same procedures had to be gone through and we were all terribly worried on his behalf. Fortunately, he was freed after thirty days of incarceration and not extradited. We were thoroughly relieved that he was out relatively quickly, but still enraged that this had happened again.

I don't know how I would have managed to readjust to my old life without Jane's support and patience. She had been there for me all through my year's imprisonment, and she was there to help me find my way back to normality as well. Our love was tested in a way most relationships never have to endure. Could any of our lives ever be the same again?

ACKNOWLEDGEMENTS

We would like thank Jason McCue and the H$_2$O Law Firm, George Clooney, Stephen Jakobi OBE, Sabine Zanker and Sara de Mas, all of Fair Trials Abroad, Baroness Ludford, Baroness Symons, Peter Skinner MEP, Caroline Lucas MEP, Graham Booth MEP, Linda Gilroy MP, Andrew Turner MP, Trevor Coleman, Carol Dennet, Alan Wells, Janet Hanson of the British Embassy in Madrid, Catherine James of the Foreign & Commonwealth Office, Charles Grey, the British Ambassador in Rabat, Anne-Marie Teeuwissen, Vice Consul in Rabat, Pascale, Nick Colyer, Hugh and Noel at Meridian, Damien Hirst, Jude, Paddy, Mariella and all the Friends of John, Jenny and friends, David and Jo, Carol and family in Plymouth, Craig and staff at Medina Boat Yard, Barry at the Duke of York, Kate and Toby Neil, Natalie, all at Hugh-Davies & Co, Dave, She-She Mum, Lil and Jon, Laura, Miles & Ned, Andrew, our mums, Frances and Leona, Francesca, Freya and Michaela for being amazing and everyone who wrote letters of support to and for John.

Forget You Had a Daughter
Doing Time in the 'Bangkok Hilton'

Sandra Gregory with Michael Tierney

Sandra Gregory was living a life in Bangkok that many only dream of – until illness, unemployment and political unrest turned it into a nightmare. Desperate to get home, she agreed to smuggle an addict's personal supply of heroin. She didn't even make it onto the plane.

In this remarkably candid memoir, Sandra Gregory tells of the events leading up to her arrest, the horrific conditions in Lard Yao prison, her trial in a language she didn't understand and how it feels to be sentenced to death. Her journey to the UK resumed some four and a half years later when she was transferred to the British prison system, where she had to adapt to a new yet equally harsh regime. Following relentless campaigning by her parents, who refused to forget they had a daughter, she was pardoned by the King of Thailand and released in 2000.

Forget You Had a Daughter is the extraordinary story of a good woman who made a mistake that changed the rest of her life.

'Amid the degradation Sandra Gregory found redemption, and the strength to rebuild the life she had thrown away.'
Mail on Sunday

Non-fiction: Memoir
978-1-904132-27-1
£6.99
www.visionpaperbacks.co.uk

FOR A HOUSE MADE OF STONE
Gina's Story

Gina French with Andrew Crofts

The extraordinary true story of a young woman from the Philippines who, aged 27, stood trial in the UK for the murder of her husband.

Even as a young child, Gina did all she could to help her family – working with her siblings on their hill farm and leaving home at 11 to become a live-in housemaid. However a series of misfortunes meant that Gina became a burden and she vowed to repay her mother and father by earning the money for them to build a stone house.

Her quest took many turns – from the fleshpots of Manila to the jet-set worlds of New York and Brunei – until she fell in love with a British man. She married him and together they had a son.

She soon realised that she was married to an abusive bully, but she agreed to move to England to salvage their relationship. Driven close to madness by her husband's violence, Gina stabbed him. Suddenly she was facing a murder charge in a foreign land where she understood little of what was going on.

For a House Made of Stone is Gina's uniquely inspiring story of love, loss, survival and hope.

'Impossible to put down.' Jane Elliott, author of *The Little Prisoner*

Non-fiction: Memoir
978-1-904132-79-0
Export isbn: 978-1-904132-80-6
UK: £16.99
US: $29.95
www.visionpaperbacks.co.uk